C000129414

Ships in Trou

Stuart Russell
and
Nigel Harris

88 Photographs
with
38 NEW to this 2nd Edition

Many published exclusively for the first time

Radio Caroline
1964-2014

50th Anniversary Edition

Ships in Troubled Waters

Nigel Harris
©2014

This book is dedicated to my mother Hazel, without whose help my escapades on the high seas would never have taken place. My sincerest thanks must also go to Terry, John, Bob, Josh and the many others who have helped me construct this book. Without their help, it would not have been possible to publish my story The first edition was published in 2009 and many generous people have purchased a copy of the book; I would like to thank you very much for parting with your hard-earned money! As you may know, a percentage of the price goes towards supporting the Ross Revenge, when obtained from the Radio Caroline webshop. If you are reading my story for the first time, I hope you enjoy it and maybe it will add some colour to your knowledge of Radio Caroline and her broadcasting sisters on the high seas. Now, very importantly, I would like to thank Marc Jacobs from Radio Mi Amigo for allowing me to use some of his personal photographs which are marked * in this updated edition of 'Ships in Troubled Waters'. Cover photo is ©*Darkrose42* (Knock Deep, 1979) To finish, I would like to add my sincere thanks to Dave Richards for his continued friendship over the years. Through all the ups and downs of daily life, and despite my ramblings, he still finds time to talk to me when many people mentioned in this book would only like to beat me up! But as the events described herein happened such a long time ago, let us all be friends when next we meet and buy each other many drinks!

Nigel

March 2014

This limited *Special Edition* of 'Ships in Troubled Waters' is available as a tribute to Radio Caroline as she celebrates her fiftieth year.

1964-2014

Introduction

This book tells the story of my journey through boarding school and onto offshore radio in the North Sea. It is not a history of Radio Caroline or offshore radio in general, nor is it an attempt to criticise any individual or group involved in the offshore ventures. It is a recollection of events from my perception only, which took place during my time on a number of radioships. As you will read, sheer dedication and strength of mind was required by all parties over the years to allow the offshore enterprises to survive. Radio Caroline was the central passion for me, as it was for so many others, and I felt it was never on the cards to give up the fight to survive at sea. Nevertheless, remembering every event, and those people involved, was difficult and I trust I do not upset anybody by telling stories they would rather forget. *(No malice is intended by anything written here!)* A few names have been left out to spare embarrassment, but I hope the narrative remains complete. Memories from my younger days are included, as I would like to think they help complete the overall picture of how I thought and behaved, and what shaped me as I grew up. Here goes so I hope you enjoy it!

(Boarding school was harsh, but the North Sea was worse)

©Nigel Harris

2014

CHAPTER 1

My journey home that spring afternoon gave me time to reflect on earlier developments. The day had not been without excitement, and now my expedition into unknown territory was nearing its conclusion.

In the wider world, the fishing fraternity was relieved as Britain's cod war with Iceland over fishing rights in the North Atlantic had finally ended in compromise. The Ramones had released their first album, laser printers were coming onto the market and the newly built Intercity 125 high speed trains were due to arrive in the UK.

James Callaghan was in 10, Downing Street and the Queen had sent the first royal email; the seventies were passing by at an expeditious rate with a new decade just a few years away.

Meanwhile, my life was undergoing considerable change and my job hunting appeared to be well under way. The most recent quest for work on this sunny afternoon had allowed me to determine a little information about an extraordinarily furtive organisation. I had visited the heart of its undercover operation housed in a small basement flat in North London, with no outside verification as to what went on behind the closed doors.

Yet, I was now on a train, speeding back to Kent, my carefully laid out strategy seemingly in ruins.

My day had started early and I was overflowing with expectation. Kissing my mum goodbye, I caught the bus to the railway station and waited for the train to London; my stomach churned slightly, but I knew I must see this obsession of mine through to its conclusion.

On arrival at my appointed destination, I'd nervously descended several raggedy concrete steps and walked along a short and tidy pathway. The path to the front door was smartly decorated with a remarkable assortment of colourful pot plants, which gave a feeling of normality to the proceedings.

Smoking a number of Benson and Hedges cigarettes on the journey to London hadn't helped, as now I felt rather nauseous. I'd fallen into the peer pressure trap only weeks earlier when I had nervously smoked my first cigarette, coughing vigorously the whole time, much to the delight of my contemporaries. Now, I needed several of these noxious things to steady my ever jangling nerves.

The investigative work that got me this far had paid off, as here I was at the secret headquarters in North London. Seeing no sign of a bell, I tapped lightly on the door. I did wish to some extent that no one would answer and I could go home again, thus saving myself any humiliation. But this would have been defeatist, so I knocked again, this time with more fortitude. The door was flung wide open almost immediately, and a boy of about fourteen stood within a small covered entrance, not a hint of a smile crossing his face. I coughed nervously.

'Hello, I'm Nigel to see Una.' He shouted back into the house, 'Mum!' and turning back to me, 'Come in, please.' The boy closed the front door as I entered the porch and walked on past me. 'Thank you,' I replied, 'it's been a long journey.' In reality, it hadn't been too bad, but I had nothing else to say and racked my brain for conversation.

The boy ushered me into a small room at the back of the house, but I found it increasingly difficult to have a tête-à-tête, and subsequently wandered across to the window overlooking a small back garden, also garlanded with colourful pot plants and flowers.

It seemed as if the boy's boredom threshold had been reached when he sighed loudly in my direction. He was of average height and thin; his face formed a slight glare as he glanced over at me, his brown hair flopping over his eyes. He swept it back on several occasions whilst walking around a large, circular dining table and on into an adjoining room. 'Mum!' he bellowed again. 'He's here!'

I put my hand into my coat pocket to check an important item. It was a cassette; a strange thing to bring to an interview, but this was an interview with a difference. This was for Radio Caroline, a pirate radio station anchored in the North Sea under the watchful glare of the authorities.

The radioship lay at anchor, some fifteen miles off the Essex coast, playing pop music to millions of fans across Europe. I wanted so much to be part of this undertaking and now I hoped to see my ambitions to be a Radio Caroline deejay realised.

The station had been a sensation back in the days when there was nothing else to listen to, apart from the rather reserved BBC output. The pirate revolution of the sixties had shaken radio broadcasting in Britain to its core.

Radio Caroline had been the first offshore station to broadcast to the United Kingdom and was followed by many imitators over the next few years, culminating in the introduction of a law designed to silence them. The *Marine Broadcasting Offences Act* arrived on the statute books in nineteen sixty-seven and effectively silenced the pirate stations except for Radio Caroline, which fell foul of creditors seven months later. The two

Caroline ships, one in the south off Felixstowe and the other in the Irish Sea off the Isle of Man, were towed away to Holland by the Dutch tendering company, Wijsmuller, in lieu of owed monies. The radioships remained in harbour for many years and their condition deteriorated considerably.

One of the two ships, the Mi Amigo, did eventually manage to get back to sea in the early seventies, this time off the coast of Holland; the other, the Fredericia, was ultimately scrapped.

The Mi Amigo returned to the English coast after Dutch legislation was passed in the mid-seventies, outlawing the several pirate stations broadcasting off Holland.

Radio Caroline, certainly to an outsider like me, was a secret organisation, although problems at sea involving anchor breaks or lifeboat rescues always made the news. I had discovered a few snippets of information about the organisation in this way, but nothing of any real substance. One account, well propagated at the time, was that the supply boats, known as tenders, sailed out to the Mi Amigo from Spain. I had no reason not to believe this, and looked forward to long breaks in the sunshine waiting to go out to the radioship.

But for now, I sat alone in a small, ordered room in a suburban house with no clue as to what lay ahead. One corner seemed to be the business end and I craned my head across, attempting to read some papers lying on the table, whilst not daring to move from my chair in case someone walked into the room. I wondered how many people lived here and what this Caroline boss was like. Would she like me, and more importantly, would she hire me?

'Through in a minute,' came a calming female voice from the corridor outside, and I felt my nerves kick in a little more. 'Tell me all about Nigel,' said Una as she walked past and into what I now knew was the kitchen. 'Tea?' And without a pause, 'Herbal is all I have, but you'll love it.'

I sat wringing my fingers. 'That'll be fine, I love herbal tea. My mother and I drink it all the time.' Inwardly, I shouted at myself for this mindless proclamation; now she'll think I'm a mummy's boy. And I hated herbal tea.

I stood up as Una came back into the room and it was only now that we really met. She was a short, slim woman, about five foot four, which made me feel far taller than my five foot ten when I stood up to greet her. She was around forty, I imagined, with a broad, slightly crooked smile and a face beaming with friendship that totally relaxed me. 'There's a deejay from the ship coming along in a minute,' she said as she went back into the kitchen. Una continued as she made the tea, raising her voice a little, 'I always get someone on shore leave to come along to help with the interviews.'

This made me a little wary and I wondered who was coming to my meeting. Just then, her son came back into the room, clutching some school books and casting me a dubious glance. Una arrived with the tea.

'Tyke, this is Nigel from, where was it?' she paused, putting down the tray. 'Remind me.'

'The Isle of Sheppey,' I replied, adding, 'in Kent.' 'Oh, right,' said Tyke in a most uninterested way. He grinned at me and shrugged.

I had found out about this office a few weeks earlier in a rather hit and miss manner. In the absence of any mention of Radio Caroline in Yellow Pages, (surprise, surprise), I had answered an advertisement in a music magazine, the New Musical Express, selling tapes of old pirate radio stations. I ordered some radio jingles and tentatively enclosed a letter intended for Ronan O'Rahilly. He was the founder of Radio Caroline and I had no idea even if he was still involved with the station.

So, I was pretty amazed when, within a month, I received a reply; my correspondence had seemingly found its mark. An unsigned letter arrived at home and I replied by return of post. Only days later, I received a phone call from a lady called Una inviting me to London with a sample of my work. But there were no samples; I had no radio experience.

With school now over and no immediate plans for further education, I was in somewhat of a quandary as to where my future lay.

I had gone to a public school in Canterbury and had already planned my future career by the age of nine. I sang in the senior school choir everyday and in the cathedral most weekends. An additional benefit to being a chorister was hearing the organ music; it was a sound I adored from a very early age.

Hence, in due course, I studied organ at school and had big plans for university as an organ scholar. The eventual outcome, I believed at the time, would be a cathedral organ post and the chance to become über *rich*. But sadly, the academic side of school let me down. Even a later appearance at technical college failed to propel me forward.

Apart from English, music, geography, divinity and the arts, I was pretty useless. But that was not my only downfall. There was a profusion of dreadful sporting activities to tolerate; again, I failed excessively.

At school, I swam, boxed and ran; I played cricket, football and rugby too. But the most terrible of sports was cross-country, held in all weather conditions. And how I loathed it. I used many tricks such as getting a bus back to school from far-flung locations and still arriving last so that nobody would suspect me of cheating. Conceivably, I wasn't so daft.

But then this ploy was not exclusively mine, as I found out one day when boarding the bus in a heavy rainstorm, only to find another ten boys from school already onboard.

On reflection, had I been more successful at school, it is certain I would not have been sitting in London on this particular afternoon, hoping for a job on Radio Caroline. It does seem that everything has a reason and as I grew older, my thoughts towards a life on the high seas aboard a radioship became stronger by the day.

A heavy pounding on the door sent Tyke scurrying from the room. He came back with the visitor from the ship, who was introduced to me as Mark Lawrence. I had heard Mark on the air many times and felt genuinely pleased to meet him. But he was not smiling, giving the impression this was a chore with which he could do without. I felt a little uncomfortable as we were introduced by Una.

Tyke left the room when his mother asked him about homework and he grunted at her from the hallway.

Una sat down at the table and uttered the dreaded sentence.

'Let's hear Nigel's tape, there's a machine over there.' I reluctantly handed my cassette to Mark who clicked open the tape player and placed it inside. Any remaining self-belief was rapidly slipping away.

I had no studio equipment of any sort at home so I had visited Tandy's, the electrical store in the high street, and bought a cheap microphone. Along with mum's record player and a cassette recorder, I'd attempted, over many days, to make a demo tape. I thought it sounded reasonable when I made it, but now my voice droned out of the tiny speaker, sounding worse than I could ever imagine. I looked down at my feet, praying that the machine would stop or the tape would snap. But no, it went on and on and I felt wretched.

A little later, I was on an underground train sitting opposite Mark whilst heading back to Victoria station. He was short and a little podgy, with messy, slightly curly, blond hair and he wore ripped jeans and a t-shirt. I had worn a suit and tie, my Sunday best for the occasion at which I had hoped to make an impression.

Una sent me home requesting another tape and I assumed this to be the brush-off. She had asked me whether I could live away from home for weeks on end and I had cited my boarding school experiences as positive evidence. 'That's not a problem,' I had said, full of hope at the time, 'I would cope well.'

Mark and I parted company further down the line and he politely said goodbye. We had hardly said a word to each other on the train.

'Never mind,' said my mum when I got back home. Always looking on the bright side, she added, 'They will call you later, I'm sure!' 'Yes, of course!' I amenably replied, soundly disappointed.

So that was it, my short introduction to Radio Caroline. I listened to the station again later that evening, thinking I could do better than the bizarre sounding hippy who was on the air at the time, but I would probably never be able to prove it.

Life now got back into its daily routine. On the work front, I heard there was a vacancy as a dental technician in town, which sadly involved making false teeth; not for me I decided. But something had to be done soon. The fallback was to reconsider my education, go back to college, and bump up my qualifications. But that was too much like hard work and I dismissed the idea.

I hadn't fared too well at school, so why should now be different? I decided to worry about it another day, as it was now the weekend and I hoped to enjoy myself a little. I rang my best friend John, whom I had met when he was helping the milkman during his school holidays. We became good friends, although he did not fully understand my radio ambitions.

I was still in bed early one morning a week later, when the phone rang. When it wasn't answered, I stumbled out of my room and into the hall.

'Good morning, this is Nigel.' 'Hello, it's Una,' came the reply.' My heart literally stopped for a second.

'Can you pop up to town this afternoon? I'd like to see if we can get you out to the ship next week.' I felt the exhilaration start building up inside me.

'But I haven't had the chance to do another tape.' 'Forget that, can you get here today?' she continued. 'No problem, I can get there after lunch. Is that okay?' 'That's perfect. I have to go across town this morning, oh, and by the way, think of a new name for yourself, will you? See you later.' She hung up and I gasped for breath. I was going to Radio Caroline; this wonderful thing I had heard so much about, and listened to so many times, was now within my reach.

I ran excitedly into mum's bedroom without knocking and jumped onto the bed, shouting with delight. If she had hoped for a weekend lie-in, it was not going to happen on that particular morning.

My mother, Hazel, had lost my father many years before. His name was John and he had been a Medway Pilot, working for Trinity House, based in Sheerness, Kent. This is the reason we ended up on the Isle of Sheppey; work rather than choice. My father had been brought up on the Isle of Skye in Scotland and was the son of the local rector. He had joined the Merchant Navy after leaving school and met my mother in a shipping agency in South Wales; they married not long afterwards. My sister Rosemary and I were the results of his infrequent visits home from sea and we actually saw very little of him as we grew up. I was then sent away to boarding school and saw even less of him.

One afternoon, he collapsed and died from a massive heart attack whilst we were walking in the front garden. Mum had gone shopping that morning and our neighbours had called for an ambulance. He had died before he hit the ground, according to the autopsy. My Auntie Hettie, mum's sister from Somerset, arrived that afternoon for a holiday, only to be greeted with the news of my father's death. Mum and I had gone to the hospital a while later as she had to identify him in the mortuary. It was a very disturbing experience.

Having endured a very strict upbringing himself, my father continued that with me. My sister, for the most part, escaped his tyrannical rule and her life continued without too much gratuitous attention.

My father bullied me severely at times, and on many an occasion he would beat me with a leather strap for some minor error. Nothing I ever seemed to do was right and he continued to find fault. He even discussed with my mother the possibility of getting me a prostitute when I was older, to make a man of me. I never found out what my mother made of all this codswallop, having only discovered the account from a relative some years later.

On several occasions, I slipped away to distance myself from heated squabbles between my mum and dad, and slept in the airing cupboard. A few times, I hid in the garden shed and crept back to my bedroom early in the morning.

I had good friends in our housekeeper, Mrs. Higgins and our gardener, Tom. Both were delightful people who treated my sister and me with great affection.

Tom, especially, was a confidant and given the chance, he and I would discuss my many problems at home and school. He was a widower and even when not required, he would turn up for work on our gardens; he relished the company, as did I.

Had my father lived longer, I don't think there would have been a chance in hell he would have allowed me to become involved with Radio Caroline; it would not have been his style.

I could not feel sad when he died, for it was such a relief that the uncertainty of my father's moods had gone from my life. There was no more feeling of dread as I waited for the sound of his key in the front door, knowing he had been in the pub all evening.

There were times when he was a very kind man and I wished these occasions could have been the predominant ones. He and my mother seemed to argue continually, mostly about me, school fees, his drinking and the huge amounts of money he spent on alcohol.

Several weeks after he died, the ugly truth dawned on me that I had lost my father, and my feelings changed; a gulf of sadness overwhelmed me and I became emotionally lost for a while and missed him greatly.

I arrived in London to see Una later that afternoon, and for a change, used a bus service to cross town rather than the underground tube. To say I was excited would be an incredible understatement; I was so eager to get going and still convinced I would be going to Spain to get to the Mi Amigo. An idea soon to be scotched.

It was herbal tea again at Una's house, but I didn't mind.

'We are short of a couple of people, Nigel,' she said. 'Any chance we can send you out on Wednesday?' 'Yes, that's fine,' I replied, trying to sound business-like and suppress my sheer delight. Una was at her small bureau on the window side of the room, pulling out sheet after sheet of typed paper from a drawer.

'Okay, this is how it works. You'll catch the ferry to Boulogne on Tuesday afternoon and go to the Hotel Alexander.'

I was leaning forward eagerly, the feeling of anticipation growing all the time. 'I will book a room for you and the guy who's going with you,' she said, pausing as she fiddled with more papers.

'You'll leave on Wednesday morning from the harbour. All the details of which boat to look for are in this envelope, along with some instructions for the boys on the ship. I'll give you the money to pay for the tender, so just hand it to our boatman, André, when you meet him.'

She paused, frowning a little as she gathered her thoughts, then continued. 'Now keep this to yourself. Two and a half thousand francs are here for the tender and also the money for your ferry crossing and hotel.

Take as little luggage with you from home as you think you'll need, it makes things so much easier. Have you come up with a new name yet?' I hesitated, then announced my decision. 'Yes, Stuart. Stuart Russell, is that okay?'

'Fine, that's great.' That was all she ventured after the many hours it had taken me to think it up; she never called me Nigel again. Secrecy was the prime factor in this company and even names had to change.

So it seemed I was going from France and there would be no chance for any sunbathing in Spain; that was a major disappointment.

'Who's coming with me?' I enquired.

Una explained. 'A word about some of the people that you'll be working with onboard. You'll meet Tony Allan in France; he's a really nice guy most of the time but does have a tendency to be a little difficult. And do you have a problem with gay people?'

'No, none what-so-ever,' I replied. She laughed, continuing, 'Good, well Tony is gay and may try it on with you; one can never tell! But be firm and do not stand for any nonsense. Oh, and there's a young gay Dutch deejay on the ship. Again, don't worry and don't do anything you don't want to do.'

The excitement of going to the ship nullified any thought of being raped in the night by rampant deejays. But nevertheless, this was another world I was entering.

I gathered up my bits from Una and felt as if the crown jewels had been handed to me.

But there was one question at the back of my mind that I had put off long enough, and that was payment.

'Any money when I come back?' That was the politest way I could think of putting it, blunt and to the point.

'I like to try and get the boys as much as I can from 'god',' said Una, with a degree of uncertainty. I frowned and looked puzzled. 'Oh, that's Ronan. Sometimes as much as twenty-five pounds a week, if it's there, but I always push for more.' She smiled as she collected some more papers and stuffed them into large brown envelopes. So this was the famous Ronan O'Rahilly who had started it all in the sixties. The man was still involved and I wondered if I would ever meet this so-called 'god.'

The door closed behind me. I was on my own now and heading to France within days; a new adventure was shortly to begin.

It was to be the start of the career that would shape the rest of my life.

CHAPTER 2

The Sealink ferry pulled into Boulogne in the early hours of Tuesday evening; the weather was overcast and drizzly. Even though it was early spring, it was a most unpleasant start to the epic days that lay ahead. I wandered through the dimly lit streets looking unsuccessfully for the Hotel Alexander. There were very few people in evidence on this dank evening, and most of the buildings displayed closed shutters, making me feel a little lonely.

My thoughts had now turned to the prospect of meeting Tony Allan; I knew what he looked like, having seen pictures of him on numerous occasions. He had been involved in Radio Caroline for many years, along with various other offshore stations, so there were countless photographs of him floating around.

I stopped to buy some frites. They were surprisingly small, very salty chips, with a foul tasting red sauce. And a coke was required too after all the walking I had endured. I looked quizzically at the vendor. 'Hotel Alexander, s'il vous plaît?' 'Ah, oui,' he replied. I thought my limited French would now well and truly be tested, but no, he just pointed across the road with a stubby finger and the hotel was right on the corner. Not a very impressive sight at first glance, but not unique either. It sat alongside several other small hotels of a similar character, all battling for the same second-rate clients. That included the Radio Caroline team, who would use it many times over the forthcoming months, not through choice, but through financial constraints.

I walked into reception and there was a man already engaged in conversation with the hotelier; it was Tony Allan. I wasn't ready for him yet and turned away, glancing through the small glass partition in the main doorway. After a moment or two, Tony got into a lift and the doors closed behind him. I now had the chance to get my admission sorted out with the concierge and placed my passport on the desk.

I checked in and discovered that Tony had asked to be informed of my arrival and on closing his admissions book, the man behind the desk picked up the phone.

'Non, non, s'il vous plaît! Une surprise pour Monsieur Allan!' I hoped the man understood me, although he wasn't pleased to be interrupted in his duty. He put both hands up and sighed in mock horror. 'Très bien, monsieur!' 'Merci,' I replied awkwardly, and stepped into the lift.

Tony and I were booked into rooms seven and eight, and when Tony heard the lift doors open, he appeared on the landing. He was smaller than I expected, not short, but wiry, even bony, with a long thin face and the typical hippy hair that I assumed came with the Caroline territory.

'You must be Stuart?' he asked and I nodded. He ushered me into his room and I placed my suitcase on the floor just inside the door. 'How is Una? She's a darling, we all love her.' He did not pause for breath before taking the initiative. 'We'll go downstairs and have a drink, and you can tell me all about yourself. C'mon, get a move on! And leave your bags in here, nobody's going to touch them.' I fumbled around with jackets and suitcases and placed my own room key on Tony's bed. 'Come on!' he repeated, and then he was out by the lift.

Neither of us possessed much money, so we drank beers in small glasses, emptied after a few swallows due to the huge amount of froth on top. Tony remained unaware of my secret money for the boat trip, and as our own cash started to run low, I knew it was a secret I must keep.

Tony remarked that he'd been living in Holland recently and had not been to the ship for a while. I listened with fascination to his stories of boarding parties on the Mi Amigo when she was off the Dutch coast, the attempted takeovers and varied endeavours to make money to pay off creditors.

His story telling was infectious and before long, I was eager to hear more. He had many stories from his first radio job on the offshore Radio Scotland when he was sixteen, and there were wide-ranging tales about Radio North Sea International in the early seventies.

A real passion for Tony was the Voice of Peace. This was an offshore radio station anchored off the coast of Tel Aviv in Israel, and Tony had spent many years working in this part of the world.

Now we got onto more pressing matters and began to discuss current events on board the Mi Amigo. Tony said he was going out to assume the position of programme controller. How authorised this position was, I wasn't sure, as Una had said nothing to me about it before I left England.

It seemed Tony knew how the system worked, for he unexpectedly insisted on knowing how much money I had been given for the tender, becoming quite shirty when I said I did not know anything about payment. I shrugged and flustered around for a while longer before stupidly admitting that I did indeed carry the cash.

Tony now put his plan into operation. His brainwave being that we should use some of the money to buy extra food for the ship after getting the price of the boat reduced. I decided there was no point lying about the amount of money I carried and told Tony that I had been given two and a half thousand francs to pay for the boat.

'That's an obscene amount of money to pay for an old fishing boat. Hand it over and I'll go down to the harbour in the morning and get us a better deal, then we can get some decent food to take with us. The Dutch only send crap supplies and Una won't mind; in fact she'll be pleased if we reduce the cost.' The tender will be cheaper next time was Tony's hypothesis, and if his plan worked, it was beneficial to all. I went along with it.

The envelope left my possession that night and in the morning Tony had, I assumed, gone to the harbour to negotiate. I checked out of the hotel, and making my way towards the seafront, found our fishing boat tied up along with many others. I introduced myself to the skipper, André, and at the appointed time, anxiously climbed on board with my luggage. We were due to leave in about half an hour; plenty of time for Tony to get back with the shopping. But Tony never did come back.

He had disappeared with the cash. I was beginning to panic quite seriously as the time to leave drew near. It was my first trip to Caroline and I'd lost the tender money, got on a boat for which I could not pay and would surely have to come up with some fairytale to tell the skipper. If I told him now, we would not sail, so it would have to wait until we were well underway, thus making it not worth his while to turn around and return to port.

The wind was a little gusty as we pulled out into the harbour basin but I hoped the journey would be fairly comfortable. We chugged alongside the other small boats still at their moorings, our wash rocking them gently against one another. Their marker-flags used for fishing, blew rapidly in the breeze, clattering together as they did so.

At last we turned out into the open sea, and it was then I found out I was not the sailor I thought. I clung onto the wheelhouse and without more ado, threw up on the deck. As we reached the harbour wall limits, we immediately hit an enormous wave, large enough to send me flying along the deck amongst the fish guts and nets.

I struggled to my feet, slipping and sliding, whilst gripping onto anything that would prevent me going over the side. This was hell and already I was desperate to get off the boat. I struggled into the small wheelhouse, but the atmosphere was so claustrophobic, I had to leave straight away and get outside. Within minutes, I was frozen to the spot and firmly gripped the side of the wheelhouse, mortified at the prospect of spending anymore time in this heaving sea. Tears streamed down my face but nobody could tell as I was drenched from head to foot in the ice cold North Sea. I could not see the horizon through the spray and did not understand why we left harbour when the weather was so dire. What was the matter with these men? The crew beckoned me inside again but I could not move from my position on deck at the side of the wheelhouse.

The prospect of drowning crossed my mind; maybe we would capsize and go down with all hands into the freezing sea.

The water was deep green, a colour I had not witnessed before at sea and most of it was above us, towering high into the darkening sky. We would ride up one side of a mountainous wave, teeter on the top, then slide down the other side, the bows of our little boat plunging under the waves before recovering and waiting for the next giant to lift us again. This boat, now setting out on its perilous and illegal journey, was small and the larger vessels in our vicinity appeared to be coping far better.

I discovered later that we only made about three knots for a good part of the trip and had I known this piece of information at the time, it would have seriously acerbated the already painful experience. It was difficult to perceive any forward motion at all, as most of the time was spent battling these dark green sea monsters.

In time, the darkness of the sky became even more menacing and this changed the hue of the water to almost black, the odd twinkling light still visible through the gloom and spray. Crewmembers kept an eye on me from the wheelhouse but even though I was distressed, I preferred to stay on the deck. Being outside in the fresh air was the preferred option on this journey.

I guessed we were about four hours or so into our trip and the seas had begun to relax their shocking grip on our little vessel. It was still bumpy but compared with the earlier part of the voyage, it was tolerable. The crew inside were not suffering to any degree as this was just another run to sea for them. As my stomach eased a little, more pressing matters came to mind again as I wondered how close we were to the Mi Amigo. I decided to ask, and then in the remaining time, work out how to tell the skipper the bad news about my financial situation. The information came back that we were barely halfway there, with the same distance to be covered again, maybe a little more. This news was not good, but at least I had time to work out my cover story. I thought I might even attempt a cup of tea and risk a quick cigarette before too much time passed.

We moved onward, now pretty uneventfully, through the darkness. The sky was littered with twinkling stars, made even more fascinating due to the movement of our boat. Flashing lights were everywhere on the sea, some close enough to make out the shape of a ship, others just specks of light, twinkling in the distance. We were crossing the busy shipping lanes of the English Channel and careful watch was kept as we moved ever closer to our target.

By now, I had worked out a way of dealing with the money crisis. I decided to inform André that I had accidentally left his money in an envelope in my hotel room and had only noticed this on arrival at the Mi Amigo. I would then tell someone leaving the ship exactly what had happened, and let Una sort out the mess.

That was the plan and shortly I would have to carry it out; it wasn't the end of the world, considering what I had already experienced on this infernal boat, although it was an added irritation.

I ventured once more into the wheelhouse but it was cramped and smelly, so again, I came outside onto the slippery deck where it remained icy cold. I was not wrapped up as well as I should have been, and was still unquestionably wet through from the earlier bad weather. All this made for a very uncomfortable remaining few hours.

There were many bright lights in the distance with some appearing brighter and closer than others. We seemed to be making for a cluster of them, so could the end be in sight? Sadly not, and I sorrowfully watched as yet another ship passed in the night.

I cupped my hands around my lighter as I lit a cigarette with difficulty and crouched down on the deck, shivering almost in time to the boat's rumbling, pulsing engine. In order to see a little more, I squinted my eyes in the ever brightening lights of a nearby ship.

I held my breath in anticipation as we moved closer, although there was no discernible decrease in our speed yet. And then suddenly, as we turned slightly, I could make out the shape of the Mi Amigo, her deckhouse lit up with two bright halogen lamps mounted on front of the bridge. We were getting ever closer and all the anguish of the last horrendous hours melted away. There she was in all her glory, the Mi Amigo. Radio Caroline was in sight, her red and black hull bathed in the lights from our tender as we pulled alongside.

People spilled out of the doorway on the portside and ropes were thrown across to the radioship to secure us. The fishing boat's engines revved again as she reversed a little and came to rest on the leeward side of the Mi Amigo, in what were now relatively calm waters.

The name *Caroline* was spelt out in blue alongside a painted bell on the deckhouse, whilst on the hull, blazed the words, *Mi Amigo*. I gazed at the huge mast as it towered upward into the dark night sky from the bows of the ship. The sight was amazing and it appeared dreamlike to be sitting alongside the m.v. Mi Amigo. 'Come on, climb over if you're staying, man,' came a voice from Caroline's deck. 'And hand your luggage over first!' I looked for the person behind these orders and saw a young man with a beard and a pom-pom hat holding his arms out for my suitcase.

The side of the Mi Amigo was not high and I could almost step across from one boat to the other when the tender rose on the swell. Handing my luggage over, I jumped onto the deck of my new home to see water barrels strewn along it. Gas bottles lashed to the deckhouse were being untied and put onboard our tender as new ones appeared from a small hold at the front.

Just for a moment, I felt a little confused. As the work between the two vessels came to the end, André climbed on board and I grabbed him by the arm as he prepared to step inside the Mi Amigo's deckhouse. I managed to make him understand the money situation, or at least my version of it. To my amazement, he did not seem too bothered, but I imagined he would be on his return to land.

I was told an American deejay would be going ashore, so my next job was to track him down, tell him what had happened to the money and offer my apologies to Una.

The boat was not alongside for long before the reverse operation took place. The undoing of ropes, some hurried goodbyes and then the tender pulled away from the Mi Amigo, the small deck lights disappearing into the night. Soon, they were completely gone and I was not envious of our American friend's journey back to land. I hoped it would be considerably calmer for him as they made their way back to France.

I briefly looked up and down the deck, took a deep breath and stepped inside the Mi Amigo; the ship about which I had dreamed for so long.

CHAPTER 3

I sat in the messroom taking in the excitement of the arrival of the tender, something I would soon learn to appreciate myself. I knew nobody yet, and that made the situation a little difficult. There was bottled Heineken beer on the table and as everyone else had one, I helped myself. A start of term atmosphere was about the place; a new beginning.

'So, welcome to Caroline,' said an American voice from behind me, 'What on earth did you want to come out here for?

I turned and replied in a stuttered, awkward manner. 'Don't know, really. Seemed a good idea!' I wasn't going to explain my childish enthusiasm to anyone. I stood up and shook hands with my new acquaintance who introduced himself as Jonathan Day. Tall and bearded with a warm smile and welcoming nature, he put names to a few faces in the room, mostly ship's crew at that point.

A man arrived in the busy messroom, and I recognised him immediately as Peter Chicago, already a legend in offshore radio. He was a well-built man with a mass a black hair and a frown. He had on ripped jeans and no more than half a torn t-shirt; he was streaked in oil and looked decidedly grumpy. It soon became clear he had expected to go ashore, but as so often happened on Caroline, nobody came to replace him, so he would have to stay a while longer.

He was chief transmitter engineer and had already been involved in offshore radio for a number of years, initially on Radio North Sea International off the Dutch coast. More recently, he had been instrumental in getting Caroline back on the air after her enforced silence following the hijacking of the two ships, years earlier.

Some people had gone to bed hours before and were up again at the sound of the tender, whilst many others had not bothered. Although I'd gone out to the ship quite quickly having been told about my new job, I found that Mark Lawrence, the deejay present at my interview, had beaten me to it, and was asleep downstairs. So too were the Dutch presenters who would be up early in the morning for Radio Mi Amigo, Caroline's Dutch language sister station.

I sat down in a corner at the end of a long dining table facing the main door. There was a smaller but similar table on the other side of the room adjacent to it. The walls were light green with square portholes down each side, two of which had their storm covers bolted down. The television sat on a shelf in a corner and the table beneath it was strewn with Dutch and Belgian newspapers including *Joepie* (Yer-pee) magazine, a Belgian version of *Smash Hits*, which I later established was published by the same man who owned the Dutch service on board, a Belgian businessman named Sylvain Tack. Old copies of the Radio Times lay strewn around on another small table, this one smothered in coffee cup stains.

Radio Mi Amigo had started several years earlier when the m.v. Mi Amigo was anchored off the Dutch coast. They paid rent to use the ship in the form of food, fuel, water and general running costs. This station operated during the daylight hours and Radio Caroline came on the air at six in the evening and ran throughout the night.

Boats from England were not running due to increased activity from the British authorities, several tenders having been apprehended over the previous few months with several prosecutions. One particular skipper who had been apprehended in Holland had been pretty liberal with his information when questioned, causing severe problems for the Caroline organisation.

My first night on board the Mi Amigo had arrived and it was time to go to bed. I would tour the boat in the morning but Jon, my new friend from the United States, took me into the studio before showing me to my cabin. I was soon to learn that everyone here had two names, a radio name and their real one. Una had asked me to use another name on the air but out here, away from the studio, real names were used and it became very confusing.

The new 'Stuart Russell' would hit the air at a time yet to be decided, but for now, I watched through the glass panels situated on each side of a wooden door that led into the Caroline studio.

This studio was downstairs at the end of a long corridor, along the sides of which were a number of cabins. Right at the very end was the discotheque, a name remaining from the Dutch coast days some years earlier, but now principally called the record library. Thousands of albums were stacked tightly around the walls on the lower level, with the seven-inch singles higher up. By the studio door were large red boxes containing Ampex reel-to-reel tapes, previously used to broadcast programmes recorded on land. This was now done on high quality cassette for convenience, as now, so many of the Dutch programmes were recorded in Spain at the Mi Amigo studios in Playa de Aro. The tapes were then driven north for the journey out to the ship from Belgium or France.

The Radio Mi Amigo offices and studios had moved to Spain after the passing of the Dutch Marine Offences Act in nineteen seventy-four, the same year that the Mi Amigo had sailed back to the British coast. At the time, the Spanish authorities had no laws in place to prohibit such broadcasting activities.

Contrary to the rumours which I had earlier believed, no tenders ever came from Spain, as the journey would have been too long and expensive. A blessing for me, considering the torture I had suffered on the trip from France.

Jon led me into the studio and introduced me to the presenter who smiled and greeted me. The radio equipment looked pretty basic I thought, with two Garrard turntables with slip mats for instant cueing of records, and two Spotmaster cart machines for jingles and commercials. The mixer was a half length Gate's Studioette desk with rotary controls, a piece of equipment I later found to be quite user friendly but had never witnessed before. On the left hand side against the wall sat a large speaker, turned down for the benefit of our conversation.

I was shown into my cabin for the night; second on the left looking back down the corridor from the studio. I chose to make the top bunk mine and thanked Jon, who then left me to get used to my new surroundings.

I could see a hatchway in the ceiling which I assumed looked up onto the deck of the ship. Too high to see through from down in the cabin, I wondered whether it was for light or possibly an escape hatch of some kind. There were clean sheets for the new incumbent already on the bed and as I stood in the small room, hemmed in by more green walls, I wondered which famous broadcasters from the old days may have used this cabin. Johnnie Walker could have been in here in the sixties or Simon Dee maybe. Even Tony Blackburn may have graced this cabin.

I undressed, putting my still damp clothes on a small chair in the corner and climbed up into my bunk. It was small and rather cramped compared to my bed at home, but most of all it was dry, and after my horrendous journey out to the ship, I felt as if I could sleep for days. As I lay in my bunk, I feared I may have succumbed to pneumonia, and shivered continuously until I drifted off to sleep.

I was woken up not long after seven o'clock in the morning by a constant knocking on the cabin door, but as I was a little disorientated, I could not accurately function. I sat up just as the main overhead light came on and walking towards the bunk was a short podgy man, unshaven and bald with grey wisps of hair around the ears. A grubby t-shirt and checked trousers really made him an odd sight first thing in the morning.

'How you want your fucking eggs, huh?' he spluttered into my face as I leant over the edge of the bunk. 'Fried or scrambled, boy?' he queried in a strange accent. I had no idea what he was on about but just muttered the words, 'Scrambled I think, please,' and he left the room. I had no idea what his first language might have been, but it certainly was not English. Sleep grabbed me back again, probably in seconds, and I woke up naturally a little later in the morning.

I emptied my suitcase onto the lower bunk and reached for clean, dry clothes. I soon learnt it did not matter what anybody looked like or dressed like or even smelt like on this ship, but I grabbed my sponge bag anyway, and went in search of a place to wash.

The shower room was at the top of the stairs which led to the galley on the left and into the messroom on the right. I showered for a few minutes only, as to linger too long in the precious fresh water was a misdemeanour according to notices all over the bathroom.

I felt so much better and ready for anything as I wandered into the messroom and looked around. It was deserted except for a caged canary, silent and balding, on the far side of the room. His name was Wilson and the poor thing was gripping the rail tightly with his little feet to compensate for the gentle movement of the ship; not too dissimilar from being up a tree in a slight breeze, or so I thought.

On the other side of the messroom was a door which led to the Dutch studios of Radio Mi Amigo. I discovered that those were the same studios used by all the big names in the sixties including Dave Lee Travis and Johnnie Walker; Tony Blackburn had been there too, along with Robbie Dale and many others. So much broadcasting history made in one little room; it was pretty daunting to contemplate.

By continuing on past the studio along a short narrow corridor, I came to a flight of metal stairs and peered down. This room was right underneath the main mast on the foredeck and housed the transmitters, which certainly were an impressive sight. The main one was a 50,000 watt Continental Electronics unit which ran mostly at half power but now and again at full strength, depending on fuel allowances. It transmitted the programmes of Radio Mi Amigo by day and Radio Caroline at night; this had been the situation for several years now. In addition to this was a 10,000 watt standby transmitter used mainly during maintenance on its bigger sister or when fuel was low and power needed to be conserved.

There had been a short-lived daytime service run by Caroline on this smaller transmitter and while it appeared again from time to time on different frequencies, it never survived for very long.

I wandered back through the messroom and along to the galley. This place was full of pots and pans hanging around the walls, large ovens on two sides with tea towels draped everywhere. A large breadboard sat to the left of a double sink, now full of breakfast dishes. Within seconds in came our chef, the man who had so politely asked about my eggs beforehand.

'What for you do in here?' he barked at me. 'I'm hungry, maybe a sandwich, or something? I asked. He was not impressed, but lifted my t-shirt and slapped my stomach. 'It's nothing in here, huh?' His stubbly face was brushing my cheek as he spoke, and I hoped he would be sympathetic and let me eat.

He walked me to the galley door and shoved me out, so I retreated to the messroom once again, picking up a magazine and settling down to flip through the pages. It was about fifteen minutes later when the door was flung open and in walked the chef with my breakfast of scrambled eggs. He plonked it down on the long table by the wall, went out again and came back with some tomato ketchup and coffee. What a good chap he was, this man with no name yet and a poor command of English.

All became clear soon. He was an Israeli, his name was Trevi and he had every Tuesday off, when he would get blind drunk and routinely threaten to leap over the side of the ship. Still, I liked him and he was always good to me, if a little too touchy-feely at times. Taking my plate back to the galley later, I was amazed to see the transformation. The place was as clean as a new pin with nothing out of place and even the floor had been scrubbed, although I found out later this was a duty shared by all and sundry at some point.

Life on board was good with plenty of fuel and water and no shortage of food or alcohol. One drawback for me was the availability of cigarettes, with cartons lying in wait for me everywhere I looked. I took the chance to indulge, and did myself no favours on that front.

Many hours were spent watching television or sleeping to relieve the monotony. For the most part, a radio show would last three or four hours, so there was a lot of time to while away.

I sat in the messroom later that day watching the news on BBC1 and as I had not yet been on the air, I was still full of apprehension at the prospect.

The Dutch programmes were mostly pre-recorded in Spain with hourly news read live on the ship. A Dutch fellow wandered in and out of the messroom, saying little as he passed me, not caring to introduce himself just yet, and obviously not overly keen on his duties. This was Bart van Leeuwen, a young deejay who had started his career on Radio Veronica several years earlier.

Still no sign of any English people yet, but I guessed they would appear later as six o'clock approached and Caroline was due on the air.

Even as I was thinking this, Trevi walked carefully into the room balancing two large trays in his arms; it was lunchtime. He placed the steaming trays down on the larger table. Pork chops, about twenty of them swimming in gravy, and string beans. More pots were brought in with mountains of mashed potato and more vegetables, followed by the plates and cutlery. I was not expecting this constant food service provided by our Israeli friend, but it was most welcome. As if by magic, the entire ship's crew appeared from all areas of this out-of-the-way home from home and settled down to eat.

Several members of the crew and some deejays sat around the tables in the messroom, the conversation loud and in two different languages. I felt a little cut off and unable to join in with the chit-chat, despite sitting in the midst of this furore.

'Hey, English boy,' shouted a young Dutch deckhand, snapping me back from my thoughts, 'You like it here?' I smiled in agreement as the first course was cleared away for pudding, pots of coffee and beer.

I retreated to my cabin after lunch to make a start on sorting out my belongings. Unexpectedly, there came a knock on the door and it opened before I could respond; in came my guide from the previous night.

Jon wandered into the cabin grinning, but still looking a little dishevelled. He said he'd slept in his clothes, a habit that happened frequently, mostly due to his laziness, he admitted. Jon was due back at university in a few weeks in New York and would be leaving the ship on the next tender, never to return.

However, the inevitable was due to happen, and I was told I would go on the air at midnight. Something I had dreamed about for so many years was almost here, but despite my joy at the prospect, I still had reservations concerning my abilities to do the job.

It was a long day with a pretty heavy swell kicking in during the late afternoon which sent the Mi Amigo rolling from side to side, accompanied by the crashing of metalwork from around the ship. Ladles in the galley hanging from their hooks created a regular pattern of noise which after a while became a predictable, tuneless symphony.

The clock ticked away remarkably slowly, ever pushing its way towards midnight. Soon it was time to prepare my very first programme on Radio Caroline. Due to some repair work in the main studio, I was to work from the spare upstairs studio that night and spent an hour or so searching through the record library, carefully selecting my albums. There was a music format in place on the station with some free choice available, but only within certain boundaries; the office in London kept a very close eye on things and very little slipped under the radar.

CHAPTER 4

It was midnight and I sat in the studio, alone and nervous, preparing for the big moment. There were two turntables with instant start, which was done using slip-mats, thus enabling me to hold the record steady, having already cued it to the appropriate point. But when I let my shaking hand off the record, the needle jumped back across the album, resulting in a long scratching sound. I had already turned the microphone on and without a thought, muttered, albeit quietly, 'Fuck!' I just about heard myself say it through the headphones as the needle found the middle of the wrong song and bounced a couple of times before settling down. My first word on Radio Caroline was the 'F' word, and my world came crashing down. Thankfully, on further investigation, it seems the expletive was inaudible to the listener, so at least there would be no repercussions.

My first show was top heavy with time checks and programme schedules, but I got a chance to play some of the music I'd heard on Caroline as I grew up with the station. The airwaves across Europe resounded to music from Steely Dan and Led Zeppelin on one hand to the Electric Light Orchestra and Peter Frampton on the other. My earlier nervousness soon turned into excitement at what I was actually doing, and my first three hours on the radio flew by.

My ability to chat on the air became more relaxed over the next few days and I curbed my enthusiasm for telling the time by hanging a large piece of paper over the studio clock. But then I started to use my watch, so that came off too.

A few days passed and I was settling in well. We had another tender later in the week, this time from Holland and it brought fuel, water, supplies and a Radio Mi Amigo crew change. I was disappointed to see the departure of one of the Dutch newsreaders as we'd become Monopoly buddies and good friends. Monopoly was great fun but unusual in the fact that it was the Dutch version with nothing on the board that I recognised. I ended up in jail everytime I went round the board, which resulted in a loud shriek from me as soon as the truth dawned.

My English colleagues included James Ross, Mark Lawrence, Tom Anderson, Roger Mathews, Nick Richards and Mike Stevens. James and Mark were already friends, having been involved a lot longer than I, but we all seemed to get on well when onboard. Tom Hardy arrived a little later along with Stevie Gordon, Bob Lawrence and Stephen Bishop.

We all had approximately the same taste in music, which gave the station a good overall sound. The music was diverse and ranged from rock to pop, reggae to blues, and an assortment of other genres thrown into the pot for good measure.

Punk music was entering the fray about this time and bands such as the Sex Pistols, Eddie and the Hot Rods, the Jam, Television and the Clash were prime examples of Caroline's output. The punk sound was pretty confrontational at times but was balanced out with groups such as America, the Eagles, Jackson Browne and Stevie Wonder. The sound of Caroline as an album station was unique and new listeners were being gained all the time.

As far as deejays went, I particularly remember Roger Mathews who had been in the RAF. There were stories afoot that he worked in the kitchens but I believe they were just vicious rumours started by me and he did in fact work in aircraft maintenance; quite how he evolved into a pirate radio deejay was never fully explained. Roger was a good fellow, large in size and with a full head of grey hair. He was from Birmingham and graciously tolerated the relentless mimicking of his accent, taking it all in good stead.

Sometimes during his programmes, he would put on especially long album tracks and make his way to the galley for a snack, then pop into the messroom, lean against the radiator by the door to warm up, and watch television. Others would soon hint that his record may have ended, but until Roger was ready, he would not venture back to the studio. He always timed it perfectly.

It had been discussed on the ship around this time that we should try to get some sort of advertising underway to raise money, and not being salesmen ourselves, Roger suggested a friend who had experience in selling. Although on this occasion, we needed somebody who realised it was against the law in the UK; a huge amount of blag was required to accomplish a very difficult task. Sadly, no more became of this venture but we did welcome one of Roger's friends, Brian Martin, onboard a few weeks later. He was a great asset to the station and became one of the regular team, occasionally presenting the popular *Caroline Roadshows* which toured venues up and down the east coast of England. Our venture into sales was put off for several months.

We got mail from home on a pretty regular basis along with instructions from the London office. Sometimes there were comments on the state of programming, although it was difficult for those in London to criticise too strongly. Presenters were required to carry on working in sometimes dire situations, so reprimands usually had to wait for shore leave.

It was quite normal if somebody wasn't wanted back on the ship, to simply rest them for a while and later, quietly drop them from the presenter's list. Much has been made of the fact that over the years nobody was ever sacked from Radio Caroline, but that is bending the truth a little; it was just never put into so many words.

Tuesday was a special day for Trevi, our cook, as it was his day off. Each week it was hoped that staff with some form of culinary skill would take over in the galley, and with some help, feed the rest of us. An assortment of crew and presenters would gather ad hoc, pots and pans at the ready and prepare for the off. Two helpers on one particular Tuesday were Dutch presenters Frank van de Mast and Hugo Meullenhof. Frank was a clumsy fellow and if there was an accident waiting to happen, he'd be involved. I don't think he ever got to grips with living on a ship. Both he and Hugo were tall and gangly and found sea life a little difficult to say the least.

These two characters were now adding to the chaos in the run up to dinner. Neither had much of a clue about cooking, and I feared both would be in trouble if ever left to fend for themselves. There was an overwhelming but complicated smell of food permeating its way around the ship on this day, and it seemed that without anyone really in charge, mayhem would soon ensue in the galley. However, we were fed on this occasion, although some Tuesdays could be a little hit and miss.

There was a heavy swell on one particular Tuesday and under the circumstances, it was uncomfortable on board. We'd eaten and the dishes lay scattered around the table waiting for someone to take the initiative and start clearing them away. Trevi liked a drink and it was only on his day off that he could indulge himself, and on this day, he had taken himself to the limits.

As we watched television, the messroom door crashed open and in stumbled Trevi, just managing to hold his balance. He escaped a bruising by grabbing the corner of the table and thus avoided hitting the floor. He looked around, eyes half closed and top denture slipping slightly, moaning a little as if in pain. His complaint seemed to be the current state of the galley, and he muttered and spluttered on and on about the mess; he was a very miffed cook.

We all looked at him wondering what his next move would be. In fact it was to be downwards. He fell to the floor, grabbing at the corner of the table again as he went over, but missing this time. One of the crew dived over to help him but he was too late to save the poor man who hit the floor in a crumpled heap. Trevi was too drunk to have felt much, I thought, and watched as he was helped to his feet. He was muttering nonsense and flailing his arms around as he was half-carried out of the room. At least his teeth stayed with him.

'Pisshead,' grunted someone under his breath and we went back to watching television. About an hour later, one of the deckhands came into the messroom to ask if anyone had seen Trevi. He said he'd taken him to his cabin at the back of the ship and on going to check on him, found he had disappeared.

The journey to the stern off the ship was a dangerous trip at times. The ladder up from the lower deck level to the bridge area was missing, as were the safety railings. Two substantial planks of wood had been secured across the gap, with nylon rope to act as railings at the side of the ship. *(See picture on page 107)* The damage had been caused when a large tug had been alongside in a heavy swell whist an anchor replacement operation had been underway. She had smacked the Mi Amigo hard on the starboard stern and as always, repairs were delayed.

It could now be a journey of extreme danger to travel to the stern, even for the fittest and most sober of people. If Trevi, in his intoxicated condition, had tried to get back into the body of the ship on his own, he was probably in the sea by now.

We all ran from the messroom to search for our miscreant. Cabins below, cabins aft, the record library and the studios were all checked. We searched the transmitter room, the generator room and all the smallest nooks and crannies of which we could think. After about half an hour, it appeared he must have fallen over the side. I felt a sickness in the pit of my stomach such as never before; I went back to the messroom and sat down. There was nobody else there and I turned off the television. In the calm of the empty room, I imagined that poor old man in the cold North Sea, floating face down, dead. What a way to go, I thought. Why did we let it happen?   But it wasn't my fault. I didn't cause it; already I was trying to distance myself from the tragedy.

'Bastard!' was the exclamation from outside on deck. 'Fucking, stupid bastard!' The profanities continued half in Dutch and half in English with others joining in as the voices got nearer. The messroom door flew open and in walked one of the crewmen, his face flushed red, veins standing out on his neck like rivers of blood.

Trevi had been found asleep in the wardrobe of one of the spare cabins at the rear of the ship. He had left his bed and made the transfer to what he thought was a more comfortable option. He'd only been found because someone had been looking for spare torch batteries as they were running low on the ship. The relief was too much to bear and I almost burst out crying at the good news. Of course, I was happy for our inebriated cook, but happy too that I need feel no guilt over a man's death.

I'd been on the ship for just over a month and it would be time to go ashore for a break in a day or two. This was something to which I was looking forward with great excitement. But shore leave depended on a number of things; the weather, naturally, but also there being enough money in the funds to send a tender. A large amount of money was required for each run out to the Mi Amigo, as these supply boats were not cheap.

Ports were policed and vessels watched as boats headed in and out of harbour. Obviously, twenty-four hour surveillance of all ports and boats was impossible and hence we were able to supply our ship. There had been arrests and all manner of trouble in continental Europe and England before I had joined Radio Caroline, but it didn't really worry me too much now.

Two days later, a rusty battered fishing boat appeared alongside in the dead of night. It was not the same boat on which I'd travelled out to the Mi Amigo, as this one was much larger and carried fuel and water. The arrival of any boat was met with an almost hysterical degree of excitement, especially if some staff were due to go on shore leave, although a degree of uncertainty hung in the air at times like this. Was there enough food and fuel to keep us going until the next tender? What were the new people coming on board going to be like? Was there any bad news from land, maybe trouble from the authorities?

On this occasion, all was well, apart from the fact that I could not go ashore. The presence of an Englishman on this particular vessel going back to France was, apparently, likely to arouse suspicion; I took this news with mixed feelings.

I was keen to get home to see my family and friends and to find out how my on air performances had been received but, by the same token, I'd made new friends onboard and would be sorry to leave them. My disappointment, however, was not too long lasting.

I had no choice in the matter and would be staying for at least another week. I didn't really mind, although I threw a tiny huff just in case anyone thought I'd gone barmy and didn't care about going off the ship. My little bit of pretend reluctance to remain onboard was rather overshadowed by the departure of our poor old Israeli cook, Trevi. He was on the deck hugging and kissing everyone in sight, his eyes bleary and tear stained through drink and emotion. He was to find work elsewhere and we did not see him back on the ship again; a decision that probably saved his life.

I'd seen hundreds of cans of Heineken lager loaded into the store locker but the door was locked now, and save for breaking in, I thought I'd settle for a cup of hot chocolate. It was well after three in the morning, and I'd been on the air until nine the previous evening, so I made my way below deck to my cabin, weary and sober.

It was difficult to get to sleep, as the noise from the deck above was continuous and varied. Pumps would start and then stop, and when they stopped, the colourful language would increase, then the pumps would start again, and so on. Onboard that particular night, fuel and water was coming in great quantity, so I did not complain about the noise. Suddenly there appeared to be as much noise below deck in the cabin areas as there was from above. I soon knew why; the beer was flowing, so naturally, I got up.

The food locker was unlocked, by whom I did not know, nor care. But there it lay before my very eyes, endless supplies of lager. This was like a mini-supermarket, only this time I could help myself and consequently, I grabbed six or seven cans and scuttled back to my cabin. Nobody saw me, so if there were any repercussions, I would be in the clear.

Next morning, I woke up, head spinning and in a slight state of confusion. I crawled out of my bunk, pulled on a pair of clean jeans, a bright yellow t-shirt and slid my sockless feet into my trainers. I glanced at my alarm clock, and it was nearly ten-thirty, but that was okay as I wasn't due on the air until teatime. There was plenty of time to wander around and catch up on any news from the night before.

Later that week another tender arrived; this time, it was the same one I'd arrived on a month or so earlier and it now looked tiny compared to the fuel boat we'd had just a few days before. It seemed my return journey would be on the same boat again and I stood on the deck watching as the little vessel came alongside and ropes were being tied. Suddenly, I caught a fleeting glance of a profile in the wheelhouse. It was someone I did not expect to see; Tony Allan was here. At the time, not really knowing too much about the Caroline ethos, I could not understand how he'd been allowed to come back, having only weeks before disappeared with two and a half thousand francs of tender money. But here he was, in all his glory; Radio Caroline being the all forgiving station.

It was then that I discovered I had been asked to stay onboard. The news hit me like a sledge hammer. Mark was going home; he'd been onboard longer than me. Although I could have gone, if I'd forced the point, I decided it was prudent to stay; so here I was, standing on deck with Tony Allan. Should I mention the money? No, I thought I had better not.

I was soon to discover that Tony had a habit of causing intimidation in the ranks; he loved it and wallowed in the results. The manner in which he would ask a question had a schoolmasterly trait to it, whereby you knew, if you got the answer wrong, there would be trouble. I tried, therefore, to avoid these situations as best I could.

Nevertheless, I had a sneaking admiration for him; he was a true professional and an accomplished performer on the air, even if some programme content could give offence. In one of Tony's shows, he branded the entire City of Canterbury as rampantly homosexual, which is probably a slight exaggeration.

Tony called a meeting; there were to be no excuses for non-attendance. The atmosphere on our little North Sea ship was soon to change.

CHAPTER 5

Tony's meetings were held in spite of bad weather and seasickness amongst the deejays. We would gather in the messroom as the ship was thrown from side to side to be bellowed at for some earlier indiscretion on the air. However, meetings were not always bad tempered affairs, but tended to be so when Tony had been drinking or sniffing something, which was fairly often. Inexperienced youngsters coming to terms with life at sea and trying to learn the rudiments of broadcasting was an extraordinary combination.

Tony seemed pleased with my broadcasting abilities for now, and told me so over dinner one evening. After these positive comments, I thought I would be spared his bellowing during the programme meetings, but it was not to be. He had me on the brink of tears later in the week as I came under attack for a piece of sloppy, unprofessional behaviour on the air.

For many deejays, the tasks involved were just too demoralising and they went home as soon as possible, whilst others would persevere, hoping the situation would improve. For several months of the year, the weather was cruel and supply boats were a rare sight on the North Sea. Isolation and seasickness were the main factors in the departure of many of those who did not return to the North Sea.

The Mi Amigo was ballasted well and could withstand quite a pounding for her age, but as a sea-going vessel, she should never have left harbour in late nineteen seventy-two; she had now been at sea for many years without any maintenance. The hull had been painted shortly before I joined but, as in all endeavours with this organisation, it had not been done properly and was not finished. Nonetheless, the ship looked nice from one side and made an impressive sight for seafarers passing on a warm summer's afternoon.

Some of those summer visitors were from the British government's Home Office department. They would charter a tug, the *Vanquisher, (see pages 113/118)* and head out into the North Sea, usually arriving just after lunch. They would do several circuits of the ship, then sail a mile or so away and take measurements of our transmission strengths and anchorage position in the Knock Deep. Cameras at the ready, they would then come in closer, take their photographs and sail around our stern, ready for another sweep.

We usually stayed inside the ship whilst all this was going on but during one visit, we decided to be brave and venture outside onto the back deck, albeit with tea-towels and baseball caps masking our identities. Who knows what the authorities made of this, for their faces remained stony and humourless as they sailed slowly past the Mi Amigo. I thought it probably made their photographs slightly more interesting and it certainly gave us something to do to relieve another monotonous afternoon. Their work completed, they would return to port in England.

Our small boat from France pulled alongside once more a week or so later and at last it was my turn to go home. Bags packed and goodbyes completed, I clambered over the side and onto the heaving deck of the little floating taxi. The swell was pretty heavy again and it was no mean task to jump at the exact moment the two decks became level and close enough. A miscalculation could mean crashing down into the deep brown churning sea. I made it after a few aborted attempts and clung to the small front mast as the two vessels became separated. We drifted astern a little in the strong current and then, engines roaring, pulled away from the Mi Amigo.

The radioship looked beautiful in the fading daylight with her powerful arc lamps lighting up the surrounding activity and shining out across the sea. Beaming down from the bridge, they appeared as two bright suns in the sky as dusk fell over the North Sea. As we pulled further away from the Mi Amigo, I felt a lump in my throat; I did not want to go. Everything I had done and thought for weeks had happened on that wonderful ship. The sheer intimacy of being in this strange offshore world, a world so different from real life, caused me to feel intense unhappiness at the impending separation. My friends were there and it was my home.

We were now away from the ship's protective cover and at the mercy of the open sea, heading into the night. And what a difference that made as our journey became more and more uncomfortable on what would be an eight hour journey back to France.

As it was my first trip back to land, I was understandably apprehensive at the prospect of walking into the arms of the local gendarmerie when stepping ashore, but the sight of the coastline was tremendous when it eventually appeared through the early morning mist. I'd been straining to see it for hours, and now, there it was on the horizon; I felt akin to an explorer discovering a new country.

As dawn broke and the coastline became more definable, my thoughts turned to home and England. I had been at sea for almost six weeks and had experienced an unbelievable adventure, but now, more mundane matters came into play; the ferry home, finding a train and buying some food. All things I had not done in many weeks.

I would have to get used to the hustle and bustle of land-based life again; using a phone, putting up with traffic congestion and crowded streets. Using money again, shopping, and seeing so many different faces everyday would surely be a challenge.

We approached the harbour and slowly sailed along the outer wall, turning towards the inner basin. We could easily get lost in the midst of the hundreds of fishing boats fairly quickly, and thus raise little suspicion as to our undercover assignment.

The port was busy with working boats coming and going about their business. It was an early Tuesday morning and the tide was high as many of the fishing boats prepared themselves for another day on the ever changing seas. We tied up halfway along the harbour wall and I sat in the wheelhouse, suitcase at the ready, waiting for my signal to leave in the so-called, 'casual manner'.

'Ok, go!' exclaimed the skipper. I stood up immediately and muttered a prepared and rehearsed, 'Au revoir, monsieur,' as I clambered onto the seawall, pulling my suitcase up after me. I promised myself that next time I would travel light and look less like someone with luggage for a round-the-world cruise. I should have heeded Una's earlier counsel to travel light.

My legs felt like jelly as I walked a few steps away from the boat, and putting my case down, I leant for a moment against a small gravel box at the side of the pathway. I swayed slightly as if I were an early morning drunkard heading home. But there was no time to lose, as I had to vacate the harbour, find a bus to the ferry terminal and get myself home. I glanced one more time out across the sea as I stood on the jetty, out to where my friends remained onboard the Mi Amigo. It all seemed so remote and I felt sad and alone.

Looking carefully around, I could see no sign of any official looking vehicles in the vicinity, so I set off for the ferry terminal.

England was much the same as when I had left; for some reason I had expected there to be huge cultural changes during my absence but soon I began to feel as if I hadn't been away at all. Mum was happy to see me but added that she'd been more than a little doubtful as I had set off all those weeks ago. She had decided to say nothing at the time because she knew I was hell-bent on my undertaking. But now, back safely and undamaged, she admitted I had made the right decision; for now, at least.

I was ordered by mum to get a haircut that afternoon, but I probably stank after my rather fishy journey home, so haircuts could wait; a long hot bath was required even more urgently.

Una rang next morning and I was asked to come up to London. Full of anticipation and with a strong desire to tell my story, I set off after lunch the following day.

I stared through the train window, past the passengers' unknowing, uncaring faces and off into the distance; the vastness of the open space had taken on new meaning since my departure from England. Fields, deep in green luxuriance, spread themselves out across the terrain. Normally, I wouldn't have given a second thought to any of this, but after weeks at sea, it took on a new significance.

I was engrossed in the simple beauty of it all as the train thundered through the countryside on its way to London. The magnificence and power of the trees as they reached upwards into a cloudless sky, dominating their surroundings as the cows below munched on their green banquet. Tractors pulling loaded trailers back to the farm and narrow lanes winding between the golden corn fields, heading off somewhere quite remote and far away. Although, long before I reached my destination, I was taking it all for granted once again, as normality started to take over.

Una gave the appearance of being overjoyed to see me, but I wondered whether she was as enthusiastic as this with everybody returning from sea. I hoped not, as her welcome made me feel special.

'Come in,' she said whilst walking away from the front door and into the kitchen. 'You sounded great!' Now I knew she was just being nice; my on air work had improved over the weeks, but I thought she exaggerated slightly.

The arrangement for my return to the ship was explained to me over tea and biscuits. I would get a phone call in about two or three weeks to let me know when I was going back to the Mi Amigo. Una said she would be seeing Ronan later in the week and would get me a small gift. This was the impractical code word for money and I was later to learn that these gifts were as frequent as snow in the desert.

It appeared, as time went on, that this elusive character, Ronan O'Rahilly, had many aliases and very seldom let anyone know where he lived and worked. I still had not met him and thought it unlikely I ever would, considering his paranoia of so many things; all governments and the departments therein caused him angst with the constant pressure put upon his cherished organisation and its staff.

I soon got back into everyday life on land, but having no work and little money made me more and more reliant on my mother. I used her car all the time and protested unfairly when she expressed a desire to go anywhere in her own vehicle.

A trip to the London office a couple of times during shore leave broke the monotony a little and on one occasion, I actually picked up my so-called cash gift. It came in a small brown envelope and was handed to me as if it were of very little importance.

'I'll try to get you a little more before you go back,' said Una, as I wondered how many times that line had been used before and not followed up. It was too embarrassing to open the envelope in her company, so as I left the house and climbed the steps to the main road, I began tearing open the envelope. Twenty-five pounds was folded neatly inside, and although I knew the pay would be pretty bad, I had expected a little more after so many weeks at sea. However, having this cash was a bonus and I would be able to have a night out before going back to the ship.

My second trip to the Mi Amigo was from Ostend in Belgium, and however glamorous it all sounded to me before becoming involved, it was becoming a nightmare as far as my journeys to the ship were concerned.

I waited around for several days as the weather raged out in the North Sea. I amused myself by walking up and down the marketplaces admiring the strange continental artefacts. Lack of money was causing a problem again as the days dragged on and on.

This time, I carried no money to pay for the tender to the ship, as I was hitching a ride on the main Belgian fuel boat. This large vessel was transporting fifty tons of fuel along with twenty tons of water and at least a month's worth of food. The prospect of travelling on this larger boat cheered me up when I thought back to the horrendous journey I had endured on my first trip.

Waking up in the hotel on the fourth day, I felt ravenous and scoffed as many croissants as I possibly could at breakfast. I had just enough money for a cup of tea in the afternoon at a small café along the street; a free water biscuit came with the tea. That was my evening meal and would have to sustain me until breakfast the next morning. We had an account at the hotel, and to keep costs down, only breakfast was included, so I prepared myself for a little weight loss before getting to the ship.

By the end of the week, there appeared to be no let up in the appalling weather. I wandered down to the harbour to look at the boats as they sat forlornly at their moorings, hiding from the stormy seas that crashed around beyond the breakwater.

I was due to get a call from the tender company when the time came to set sail, but even as I prepared myself for an even longer wait, proceedings were about to speed up.

Next morning, the phone in my room buzzed several times as I lay deep in sleep. I rubbed my eyes and looked at my watch; it was half past seven. This was the call for which I had been waiting and I was told to report to the harbour within the hour.

Relief that the monotony of the long wait was about to be extinguished was a good feeling. But as I opened the blinds and looked out across the street and beyond the beach, I could still see mountainous waves out to sea.

I couldn't believe we were to set sail in this weather and my stomach heaved in stricken anticipation of the event; there appeared to be nothing I could do to get out of the impending journey

I packed up my belongings and went downstairs. This morning, I had no appetite, so as I checked out of the hotel, I peered into the dining room where only twenty-four hours before, I'd been having breakfast and feeling a lot more cheerful.

It was a short walk down to the harbour and the boat that would ferry me out to the Mi Amigo. A journey lay ahead that would be sheer hell if the seas stayed in their current condition. I climbed aboard and introduced myself to the crew.

'Are you sure we are going out today?' I inquired, knowing full well the answer, but hoping for some kind of delay. The captain was a large man with several patterned tattoos on his hands and arms. His eyes never met mine once as he surveyed his bridge; I stood looking out to sea.

'Of course, we go this morning. The weather by the Mi Amigo is good when we get there, so we can leave now.' I sat down in the main cabin behind the bridge, my head in my hands. I wasn't cut out for this and I was on the point of tears, not wanting to go through with it. Within the hour, we were untying and pulling out of Ostend harbour and along the breakwater. I looked at the weather-beaten faces around me as everyone got on with their assigned job. I felt totally isolated and frightened.

We turned the corner at the end of the harbour wall and were suddenly at the mercy of the sea's fury. The bows of the fishing boat were immediately sent plunging and I grabbed onto a metal pole that ran up from the middle deck onto the upper deck. I was breathing deeply and quickly with my eyes shut, waiting for the first jabs of seasickness to kick into play. I thought if I could concentrate hard enough, I could beat the sickness, but the more I thought about crushing it, the worse it became. We were being flung up and down on the North Sea rollercoaster from hell. Crashing from wave to wave without mercy, I felt I could stand it no more. The crew were going about their normal sea-going business; laughing and joking, even eating, as they rolled from side to side in front of me.

We'd been at sea for less than ten minutes when the first sensations of vomit began to irritate my throat and the foul taste entered my mouth. With no further warning, I threw up violently as I clung to my metal post. This was greeted with sighs of revolt and laughter from the crew. Even as I drew breath, I was sick again, accompanied by more groans from the crew. A bucket was thrown down in front of me as a burly Belgian flung a mop across my mess.

In my now frantic state, it didn't matter that we were heading out to sea and I fought my way to the deck as the vessel careered around. I was greeted by ice-cold salty spray across my face and a ferociously raw wind; the massive seas churned all around us, dark and green with the tops breaking into white flurries. Clinging to the side, I gazed across at the disappearing land and felt a desperate urge to get off the fishing boat. Just as these foolish thoughts were spinning in my head, a crewmember pulled me off the deck and back inside the deck house with such force that I almost heaved up again. The jolt backwards was so sudden and unexpected that I began to feel faint as I was hauled back to my seat near the pole.

'I have seen it before, they want to jump over the side when they feel sick!' said a crewman for my benefit, as I flinched at the closeness of his mouth when he spoke. I sat down facing the pole, whilst my arms were pulled around it and tied at the wrists with plastic bands so that I could no longer be a danger to myself. The bucket remained with me, now jammed between my feet, and I stared at it, feeling utterly miserable.

My head was throbbing and my throat sore and although I tried being sick so many more times in the next hour, there was nothing left inside me. I felt as if my insides had been torn from my body; it was an episode in my life that I remember to this day with anguish and horror.

By the time we saw the Mi Amigo, the storm had died down and the sea was indeed calm; the captain had been right. Although, I did wish we had left port a little later so I could have been spared all the grief and suffering, along with my confused plan to escape by diving over the side of the boat.

I really wonder if I would have done it had I not been taken back inside the boat so quickly. I'll never know, but the mind plays funny tricks when the body is in such distress.

Being on the Mi Amigo felt like dry land and never have I been so happy to complete a journey. Nevertheless, I was feeling very frail and decided the best thing to do was to get some sleep and hope things looked better in the morning.

I settled back in fairly well and it became a little like going back to boarding school, apart from the horrendous journeys on the North Sea, from which I seemed to have suffered on both my trips to the ship.

Each week, a tender would arrive with programme tapes for Radio Mi Amigo and other items required onboard the ship. If a boat was not scheduled or the weather was too rough, then a small light aircraft would appear, buzz the ship a couple of times and then drop a well insulated package into the sea which would bob up and down in its buoyancy float and await the rubberboat which would be launched from the Mi Amigo.

This boat trip was always a precarious affair at the best of times. If the small boat had been well maintained and better serviced, there would have been far less apprehension from those forced to use it. However in the offshore radio tradition, this was not the case. Servicing of the engine was almost non-existent and the rubberboat usually had a tendency to leak.

One particular afternoon, the Mi Amigo's crew had enjoyed a prolonged period of alcohol abuse. I had woken up late in the day and gone upstairs to the messroom only to find that a drinking competition had been taking place since lunchtime, and Radio Mi Amigo was running non-stop music, the pre-recorded shows having finished. The presenters and one of the crew were almost incapable of speech let alone anything else, so with the time nearing six in the evening, I loaded the next pre-recorded show, the Juke Box with Stan Haag, into the tape machine and set things going.

Now, that alone would have been fine, but as I made a cup of tea in the galley, the plane from Belgium appeared and having buzzed the ship a couple of times, our visitors waited for the rubberboat to put to sea. The package would then be thrown out of the plane as near the rubberboat as possible. In theory, this was a good idea, but in rough weather or when the rubberboat's engine was a bit dodgy, it was a worrying event.

The drunken crew member and one of the Mi Amigo deejays were lowering the rubberboat into the sea on the winch and as the boat touched the water, the heavy swell was throwing it back, making it very difficult to control. Others had gone out onto the deck, but any assistance was limited due to their alcohol intake and being the only sober person present, I tried to be of as much help as I could.

Two of the team were in the boat already as I clambered over the side to join them and with the ropes undone, we headed away from the ship to await the drop. None of us were wearing lifejackets and naïvely did not realise what peril we were placing ourselves in each time we left the Mi Amigo. To us, it was just a game, a very dangerous game.

There was a heavy swell on the North Sea that evening and the inflatable craft slapped hard into the waves, the spray soaking us to the skin in moments. We tried to skirt around the larger waves but did not succeed on most occasions, clinging on for dear life as the tiny boat crashed around.

Eventually, the package came tumbling from the sky, landing several hundred feet to our stern having been caught by the gusting wind. We spun round far too quickly and were nearly pitched into the sea before making our way to the bobbing consignment. Pulling the package from the water was my job, as I was least likely to fall in whilst leaning over the side. Then we were on our way back to the ship through the choppy waters, the engine having held out on this occasion. Another week's worth of Radio Mi Amigo programme tapes were safely onboard.

CHAPTER 6

Having left the Mi Amigo a few weeks later, I was soon on my way home again. The ferry back to the England gave me time for a little reflection and I thought back to the last few weeks on the Mi Amigo, wondering how long the adventure would last.

It was late morning and a light sea mist still hung in the air as we steamed out across the Channel. As the White Cliffs of Dover came into view, I began looking forward to my trip to London, which I knew would follow within days. Thus, I arrived at the Caroline office, having received the call a day later.

Una was a pleasant lady and I had warmed to her at our first meeting and today she was no less friendly. She thought I had been a star out on the *Lady*, as we affectionately called the Mi Amigo. Ronan was cheered on by the fact I had taken to the whole situation with reasonable ease and he saw some potential in Stuart Russell, an opinion that was good to hear; my job seemed safe for now.

There were lengthy discussions that afternoon about life on the ship. Una had never been to the Mi Amigo and was as intrigued as anyone could be as to the goings on out on the North Sea. Of great interest to all on land was the sexual activity amongst staff and crew on the ship; the rumour machine was in high drive for most of the time.

Una seemed a tad concerned that I had fallen victim to, what she now termed, predatory homosexuals whilst at sea; I assured her I could look after myself, so there was no need to be worried. However, any discovered indiscretions amongst the staff onboard, male or female, were seized upon and immediately made public. Despite this fact, Una got precious little out of me on this visit and I left clutching my precious twenty-five pounds.

The lack of money did not matter too much as my mother was my bill payer and landlady; a landlady who did not charge rent. I felt no particular guilt as it was just a furtherance of what had always gone on before. In any case, she did not have to fork out any funds for a day or two now, as I had a modest amount of money. My disrespectful conclusion was that she should be grateful for small mercies.

I was going back to the ship for another stint the following month, so had time to enjoy my shore leave with use of a brand new car; mum's car, no less. I recognise now that it was only with great reluctance that she allowed me to drive it.

In those early Caroline days, I was just a deejay and would use mum's new mini, Hilda, only for running around locally. In later years, things would get a little more international and complicated for the poor vehicle.

I rang Una one morning a week into my shore leave for a chat, only to be told that the ship was in serious trouble. Heavy seas had crashed into the Mi Amigo, causing widespread damage to the main deck structure and extensive flooding below. To make matters worse, the anchor chain had broken that morning and the ship had drifted inside British territorial waters before the emergency anchor could be dropped. I felt helpless and longed to be out there with my friends. Una was frantic with worry for her boys on the ship and was in a frightful state. Ronan was in touch with the Dutch team who were getting tugs organised to go and pull the ship back into international waters. It had been several years since the Mi Amigo's main engine had run properly and now it had fallen into disrepair. It was yet another project on the long list awaiting the funds required for work to be carried out.

The radio station had gone off the air and it was now a race against time to get to the Mi Amigo and move her before the authorities took action; it was a difficult and long day for all.

The Dutch radio crew left the ship when their tender arrived on the scene, fearing a British police raid. There remained onboard an English crew of Peter Chicago, Mark Lawrence and Ed Foster who managed to keep the ship afloat until a tug duly arrived from Holland a day later with the new anchor. The Mi Amigo was towed back to her original position and safety.

I discovered later just how serious the problem had been when giant waves hit the radioship; they were powerful enough to crash through heavy portholes and flood the interior. Those brave souls who remained on board had saved the ship and without them, the Mi Amigo would unquestionably have been lost.

The day dawned when I was due back on board and having been to London to collect records, scripts and money to buy food and pay for the tender from France, I bade farewell to my mum and set off yet again on a gruelling journey to the ship. I headed for France, taking the ferry across the Channel and set about my task of finding the tender, moored amongst hundreds of almost identical boats.

As usual, having rushed to get to Calais, the tender was again delayed by bad weather and I settled down for the wait. The boredom of trying to kill so many hours in the day when I knew nobody and had little money, was excruciating. Some American evangelists, who befriended me in the town, became my best friends and I made a bee-line for them each morning. They were people to whom I could speak and feel like a human being, rather than just languish about the town. However, I could not let them know my secret destination, and I felt like a little James Bond on an important mission.

The tender trip to the Mi Amigo this time was particularly uneventful, although long and boring. The regular chuffing sound of the boat's engine soon lulled me off to sleep as I sat in the wheelhouse.

The English and Dutch teams on the radioship both possessed several courageous individuals who came out to the ship on a regular basis, but there were many whom we never saw again, as it could be a very difficult and scary operation on occasions.

Once in a while we would get someone onboard who most of us would remember for a lifetime. On this occasion it was to be Samantha Dubois. She was an old Caroline hand, going back several years, and had been on the ship when it was off the Dutch coast in the early seventies. She was Peter Chicago's girlfriend and as such, unattainable to those who might have wished to have a liaison with her. Although the relationship appeared tenuous at times, Peter was a jealous man; he had every reason so to be, with a batch of rampant old sea-dogs spending many weeks at sea, isolated from the opposite sex.

Several of the deejays and crew were happy to have sex with anything that moved, with 'any port in a storm' being an apt expression. I got hauled into a drama, not of my doing, at dinner one evening when Samantha announced after a string of insulting remarks between her and Peter, that she and I were having an affair.

'Oh no, please don't say that, Sam,' I pleaded. 'I wouldn't, Peter!' He scowled at me, and said nothing. Samantha found my squirming hilarious and was in fits of laughter. Despite more protestations from me, the damage had been done and Peter and I had a frosty relationship for a day or two. He remained cool towards me at times throughout my Caroline career and I don't think he was ever my biggest fan.

Samantha was my best friend. We laughed until we cried at times and to this day, I can still see her face beaming at me from across the table as we joked our way through dinner. She had spent a long time in New Zealand before coming back to Holland to live with her grandmother, and spoke Dutch and English with a Kiwi accent. Nothing seemed out of bounds to her and I have met few people who made such an impression on me.

I was play-fighting in the messroom one afternoon and losing the fight when I thought it best to just shout for help. The Belgian sailor, with whom I was embroiled, was getting the better of me.

'Help! Help!' I screamed from the messroom floor. Samantha, who had been washing in the bathroom outside, rushed into the room, stark naked apart from a skimpy pair of knickers and offering help. Not many friends would do that

I think she had a thing about nakedness, as one morning the captain came into the studio to tell me the main anchor chain had broken. Nothing serious, as the spare one would be dropped at any time; it was not too rough, although we were riding a pretty high swell.

When the anchor chain had broken earlier in the year, the new chain had unfortunately been too short and the ship had been tugging on it in the high swells; now it had broken down near the seabed.

The captain told me not to mention it on the air, and popped his head round each cabin door to tell people not to worry, as the ship had started to roll quiet unpleasantly. Samantha got straight out of bed and came and sat in the studio with me, wearing only her briefs, and announced that she would not appear in this semi-naked condition to anyone else onboard, including her boyfriend, Peter Chicago. 'You should be honoured,' she announced.

My first reaction was to stare but because of the close proximity of her bosoms, I thought it better to look directly ahead and keep my eyes fixed on the wall clock. Of course, I could not keep this up for long and when she spoke, my eyes went from her face to her breasts and back again, as she sat alongside the desk in the studio.

We chatted between the songs as the ship was being re-anchored and the relentless rolling in the heavy swell eased.

This state of undress that Samantha enjoyed so much was again to manifest itself when the Home Office visited the ship on one of their spying missions. Several of us wore our disguises on deck as their tug approached, but Samantha decided not to bother with a mask to hide her identity, and treated the men from the ministry with a flash of her boobs as they passed the Mi Amigo on their chartered tug. Those photographs, amongst so many others taken of our ship by the authorities, will be in government files somewhere, even to this day. *(page118)*

It was just after lunch later that week when a yell came from the deck as we were watching the news on television.

'Tender!' Again someone called, and we all ran out onto the deck. We were not expecting a boat that week and became over excited as the small vessel came alongside.

The first thing we always did was look for familiar faces amongst the arriving party, and this time, there was Tony Allan standing on the shallow deck as it bobbed alongside the Mi Amigo. I had experienced his topsy-turvy behaviour on my first trip, and wondered what was in store this time. Now he was back and I was feeling cautious about the uncertain weeks that lay ahead. I had only been onboard a short while and knew that Tony was likely to be on the ship for many weeks. I went into the messroom and sat down with a beer, as did several others. Tony came in within moments, and I jumped up showing some sham pleasure at his arrival. 'Darlings,' he said, looking around at the small assembly. He grabbed a beer from the table and sat down.

Tony was in a good mood for several days, very helpful in fact, and I had started to relax around him, but one afternoon it all changed. We were sitting in the messroom watching the lunchtime news and Tony got up and left the room. A minute or two later he came back in, turned the television off and launched into a question and answer session about radio. Suddenly it was my turn.

'Nigel, who is on Radio One at the moment?' I did not have the faintest idea and told him so. He exploded at me without pausing, 'If we are to be any sort of competition to that crap, we must know what they are doing, who is doing it and why. How the fuck else can we compete, you fucking idiot. Fuck off out of here, and find out!' This tirade went on for a good few minutes and I was getting very agitated. I could have told him anything, for there was a fair chance he did not know either. With hindsight, I should have told him to shut up, gone out on deck and had a beer, as others would have done.

It was a hot summer's morning and I was up early. Several of us decided it would be prudent to get away from the ship for a while in the rubberboat. A jaunt off towards a small group of yachts sailing close by seemed a perfect idea in this bright sunshine. The rubber inflatable was lowered into the water; an easy job as the sea was as flat as a millpond. We eagerly climbed aboard as some food and drink was passed over from the deck of the Mi Amigo. Before we had a chance to untie the ropes and head away from the ship, Tony Allan appeared and looked down at us with annoyance etched upon his face. 'What's the matter, Tony?' I asked.

'Get out of that fucking boat, the lot of you, now!' He was absolutely furious and I had no idea why, or what we had done wrong. As the others clambered back up onto the Mi Amigo, Tony announced he would take the boat himself and get away for a while. I decided this was palpably unfair to the rest of us, and set about aborting Tony's endeavours.

He was unsteady on his feet, probably the result of an over-indulgence of some kind, and his dithering gave me time to loosen the spark plugs in the outboard engine. This would prevent it starting, and we would have our revenge as he, too, clambered back onboard. Unfortunately, I did not loosen them enough, and the engine started with ease. Tony twisted the throttle and sped away from the ship as I stood on the Mi Amigo's deck, puzzled.

I walked back into the messroom, disappointed at the outcome of the whole affair and sat down to watch television. Within the hour, one of the other English deejays asked me to come to the bridge and have a look over at a marker buoy, several miles away. Through the binoculars, I could just make out the shape of a tiny rubberboat floating nearby; it was Tony, drifting in the strong currents with no sign of power from the outboard motor. The spark plugs had worked lose, and the engine had failed. Tony would have no idea what had happened and therefore be unable to rectify the situation. He very quickly drifted out of sight and I stared across the flat, calm sea, unsure of what to do next.

A call to the coastguard was a necessity and that was accomplished with all haste. As we were giving details of our situation over the emergency channel, another vessel broke into the conversation with the announcement that they had picked up a man in an inflatable, drifting with no power. The ship's radio officer said the man was well, although a little vague about his predicament, but they would take him into Harwich. It was a journey back to the UK that Tony was not expecting, but at least he was okay. And we had some peace onboard.

Early one evening, a week or so later, a new arrival came onto the ship at a time when we were short of staff, food, water and fuel. The sight of a boat on the horizon had the crew of the Mi Amigo extremely excited and we all craned over the side of the ship as the vessel drew alongside. Sadly, it was not the large fuel carrier we were expecting; just some food, water, programme tapes and spare parts for the generators.

I was lazy when it came to tying up boats, my philosophy being, if there was someone else to do it, why bother. It was a messy job with orders, often in Dutch or French, being screamed around the deck, the words sometimes lost in the wind.

Unless it was perfectly calm, the two boats were always at odds with one another and to this end, I had learned to be invisible at such times. However, I must not totally undersell myself, for on many occasions I was the only one able to do the job and often found myself embroiled in the melange on deck.

On this afternoon, lots of willing hands outside meant I stayed in the messroom watching television. It was, however, only slightly more interesting than tying up boats, but far less exhausting. I sat in my usual position with my legs up and stretched out on the table. Very unsociable and rude, but I was alone on this occasion. The new crew had arrived and into the messroom came Herman de Graaf, a new Radio Mi Amigo presenter. I looked up and prepared to stand to say hello and give him some kind of welcome. But I was too late and he grabbed my ankles, swinging me round and out of the way, whilst making a vulgar comment in my ear. In due course, Herman settled in and was a pretty good colleague, apart from the fact he was permanently horny, and always on the lookout for a willing male partner.

The Dutch were an integral part of Radio Caroline and although they had their own station in Radio Mi Amigo, they realised that Caroline had something special about it. We continued to have friendly banter on the ship as to who exactly ran the show. We always reached a compromise; the English owned the ship and the Dutch paid the bills. It was, in reality, far more complicated than that simple assumption.

Difficulties arrived a few weeks into my stint on the ship in the form of another new Dutch deejay, who was to cause me much angst. This fellow took a particular shine to me, badgering me constantly to have sex with him, much to the mirth of the rest of the crew and over several months, I was to receive unsolicited gifts whenever he returned to the ship from shore leave.

It was relentless and went well beyond a joke. Very soon, I became exceptionally annoyed at the situation. One afternoon as I slept, my aficionado came into my cabin and climbed into bed with me, the passionate demands to give in starting once again in earnest. As my strongly worded protests began once more, there was a knock on the door and in strode Peter Chicago to wake me for dinner.

'Oops, sorry!' he gasped, on seeing the unexpected sight that lay before him. Closing the door quickly, he left, whilst I irritably removed the unwanted perpetrator and went up to dinner to face an awkward situation and much merriment from my colleagues. Denials of any sex having taken place were brushed aside with much amusement and ribaldry.

Also from Radio Mi Amigo was Marc Jacobs, a very ostentatious Dutch presenter who spoke English with a strong American accent, picked up after living in America for some time. He had a most infectious laugh, guaranteed to lighten any situation, and became a good friend. Marc was always ready to have a bit of fun, and there were many instances when the good of the station would suffer so that we could just enjoy some much needed exhilaration. Bags of flour were tipped over djs and crew, r o t t e n fish were dropped on their heads from above, and their clothing totally removed from the bathroom whilst they showered.

It was summertime, the weather was incredibly hot and some of the crew had grown restless, which led to tension and tantrums. Practical jokes were one way of relieving the strain and to this end, Peter Chicago concocted a potentially dangerous episode involving an oxyacetylene-filled balloon and a cigarette. A tiny hole in the deck housing outside the Dutch studio enabled a thin rod to be pushed through and under the mixer with the cigarette tied to the end. This would then ignite the gas-filled balloon that had earlier been attached under the mixer. Marc Jacobs was on the air on Radio Mi Amigo and we timed the incursion to coincide with one of his links. The ignition caused a massive explosion and years of dust and mess were blown out from under the panel in the studio.

Apart from the blast, all we heard was a continued series of expletives emanating from the studio, and so did listeners all over Europe. No damage was done to the studio, but Marc's eardrums took a battering and the unfortunate listeners must have wondered what the dickens was going on until it was explained to them later by a submissive Marc Jacobs.

One evening, I foolishly squirted Fairy Liquid through a tiny hole that led from the galley into the bathroom, while an English deejay, Mike Stevens, was showering. He was very proud of his long flowing locks and as usual, fresh water was in short supply on the ship. My aim was perfect and the fierce jet of washing up liquid landed directly in his hair. Sadly for Mike, there was not enough fresh water to rinse all the soap out, and sea water was the only solution. This made his hair very dry and spiky, and I suffered the wrath of a very irritated deejay.

For a while, there was an English cook onboard called Paul. He was an amiable chap and he and I appeared to get along reasonably well. This long hot weather seemed to be going on forever and the alcohol had run out, but there were still cigarettes for those who needed them; our main quandary was the boredom. After we finished on the air, there was little to do, some options being to sunbathe or play in the rubberboat. This particular day, I decided it would be prudent to clean the bathroom and toilet areas which were on the upper deck between the messroom and the galley.

I was a very naïve young man in my early Caroline days and a smidgen lazy too. Rather than scrub and rinse the whole bathroom, I thought it would be a good idea to tip ammonia all over the showers, washroom and toilets, with the idea of going back later to wash it all away. I closed the windows and doors after my work and went away to watch television. I soon forgot all about my cleaning endeavours and went about my daily routine of eating, drinking and generally playing around.

Having finished lunch, I decided on a nap in my cabin. As I stood up to leave the messroom, the door burst open and in staggered Paul, bent double, his face contorted in agony, eyes streaming and barely able to breath. He grabbed at a water jug on the table and poured it into his mouth, regaining his breath after several minutes. To my horror, I realised he had sauntered into the bathroom and taken the full force of the ammonia which had lain there for nearly two hours.

He was incandescent with rage and demanded to know who was responsible; I shrugged and feigned innocence. The others in the messroom knew I had been cleaning, but until now, nobody had been into the bathroom. They all looked at me and that gave Paul all the evidence he required and he came for me, grabbing me around the throat. I struggled free in seconds, essentially because Paul was not yet up to full strength, and I ran out onto the deck. He followed, but I decided to give myself up. I knew I had been stupid and done something really silly and the whole episode could have turned out a lot worse. I walked forward holding my arms out in case he made a lunge for me. 'I'm so sorry', I pleaded. 'I was stupid, I didn't think. Are you alright?'

Through the spluttering and coughing, Paul stated that when he got ashore, he would have me arrested for attempted murder. He was absolutely enraged and no matter how I pleaded, he would not be persuaded that I had not tried to kill him or others. My act of stupidity was to cost me dearly it seemed, and not knowing what else to say, I slunk away to my cabin.

Paul refused to let me eat any of the food he prepared that night so I had to fend for myself and however sorry I felt, the rest of the ship found it highly amusing. But I was more worried that my freedom was at stake when I got ashore.

It was to be another two weeks before Paul left the Mi Amigo. I stayed on board for obvious reasons and was glad to see the back of him, as he never uttered another word to me. Needless to say, he reported me to the office and I left the ship a week later. Fortunately, the whole affair was soon forgotten.

CHAPTER 7

The flagship programme of Radio Mi Amigo's daytime output was a show called *Baken 16*, named after a beacon which lay some miles from the ship, marking a sandbank. This live show was chaotic fun and we always looked forward to it, especially when presented by Marc Jacobs. Even whilst on shore leave, I would listen to it avidly and long to be there. It was broadcast at lunchtime and the English deejays would be welcome to come in and read the weather in Dutch, typically not very well. One of our team, James Ross, was always very entertaining and would head off into the weather report with great aplomb. It proved to be very popular with listeners on both sides of the North Sea and was a programme well ahead of its time. A forerunner of the 'zoo format', it eventually became open house for the entire ship's crew.

After I had been on shore leave for about ten days, I got a call from the office asking me to go back to the ship. Several of the crew were desperate to come ashore and I was to meet the new Caroline crew in Belgium and head to the ship from Ostend. I was more than happy this time because Samantha was coming back and I always believed that Radio Caroline and Samantha Dubois went together hand-in-hand. The night before I left England, I went out and enjoyed myself a little too much, given the fact I was due to travel the next day. My mother was roped in yet again to take me to the ferry for my crossing, and for her sake, I put on a brave face to cover up an horrendous hangover.

It was the school summer holidays; the ferry was full of boisterous children and their exasperated parents. I headed for the bar hoping hair-of -the-dog might tame my throbbing head.

On Radio Caroline, we had secrecy drummed into us at every turn; it was our guiding mandate. I sat alone at a window table, nursing a large vodka and staring out to sea for the majority of the journey. No conversations about my occupation or routine were allowed.

I was pleased to see Samantha and knew that we would have a great deal of fun throughout the ride to the ship. First things first and a trip to the tender skipper gave us the news we dreaded; we could not leave until the next evening. Nor could we find the other two fellows who were due to come with us and that was annoying. Missing staff was a problem from time to time, so we were not too surprised by the turn of events. The absent lads had probably changed their minds or been delayed somewhere.

Samantha and I now had to find a hotel for the night and so set off on our quest, scouring the backstreets of Ostend. The usual lack of cash kept our options to a minimal level and we found the best we could afford. We could tell even before entering the building that it was one of the tackiest venues in town. We were not disappointed either and when we climbed the stairs and entered the room, we walked into a plague of flies. It was probably the most disgusting sight I've ever seen on entering a room. I'd rather have slept in an empty water tank on the Mi Amigo, given the choice.

As we'd already paid, the chances of getting our money back were slim so the best idea was to obtain a can of fly spray from the man downstairs, empty it into the room, then leave for several hours, hoping for the best.

We walked about for an hour or so before going for a drink. No money for food, but alcohol, we could stretch to that.

Radio Mi Amigo was very popular in Belgium and many stores and bars would have it on all the time. That meant Caroline would sometimes be left on the radio after Mi Amigo ceased broadcasting for the day, as was the case tonight in a bar we found near the harbour front.

At eight o'clock in the evening, code numbers were read out on Caroline. These numbers corresponded to certain items required or situations relevant to the ship. Emergencies could then, in theory, be dealt with, without the authorities becoming aware. I knew the codes almost off by heart and tonight's came as no surprise. Numbers 40, 41, 52 and 57 were read out in a monotonous drone from someone who had clearly had enough. These numbers represented 'tender required urgently, crew members need to leave ship and water and fuel low'.

We were walking back to the hotel past the frites stalls and traders still making a late evening franc or two, when I needed the loo and looked for a place to relieve myself. There were too many people around for a random leak so we walked on until my moaning became too much for Samantha. 'Down there,' and she pointed to a hotel with a short alleyway alongside it and a public toilet at the end. I was overjoyed and ran towards my salvation.

I wandered in past a small table with a little saucer on it; a monetary donation was obviously required. There was nobody in attendance as I entered the toilet, so I did not bother to donate any loose change. I did, however, think the urinals were rather high as I stood on tiptoe at the one nearest the door. As I finished, a short, podgy woman wandered in and on seeing me, let out a piercing screech. I zipped up quickly and dashed out past the table, now with a petite old lady sitting there, looking as shocked as the woman in the toilet. It wasn't until I really gave the matter some thought that I realised I had been in the ladies loo, and inadvertently peed in the sink. The event was too embarrassing to dwell on, but I wondered what thoughts were going through the minds of the women I'd so brutally scarred.

The journey out to the ship next day was pretty uneventful and the weather remained fine. Sadly, I had picked up the smoking habit a little more seriously than before, and we rifled through our luggage no more than ten minutes out to sea in the search of cigarettes. We were the only two to make the tender on this occasion and I never heard any news about the other two people who were due to join us.

I really loved the Mi Amigo and was overjoyed when she came into view about seven long hours later. It was never particularly easy coming alongside and we made several attempts on this occasion to get the tender in the right position to catch the ropes being thrown to us.

Both Samantha and I clambered onto the ship and made our way into the mess room. Always first to question any incoming crew were those hoping to go ashore. This time was no exception and we were bombarded with questions and requests to go home. I said that sadly, on this occasion, no one was to leave, as more crew were due in a few days. I knew this to be a lie, as I did not really know, but I was becoming part of the Caroline 'cabinet' and spoke the party lines. At any rate, two deejays had not made the tender, so we needed all hands.

A regular team of deejays was now reasonably established on Radio Caroline, although we did continue to see a few individuals on the ship for just the one trip. They were either seasick for much of the time or decided that radio from a ship was not their forté.

The company soon started to run people to the Mi Amigo from England once more, which was a blessing as the journeys from the continent were long and arduous. This change meant a trip to Brightlingsea in Essex for the three or four hour journey to the ship. Only people and small amounts of food and equipment could come from England due to the size of the craft used.

These boats were organised through a couple of hardcore Caroline supporters from Suffolk who adored the station and nothing was too difficult for them. Over the years, they became folk heroes and Albert and Georgina were our heroes on board the Mi Amigo; they were our contact with home. We had used a Spanish address for our private mail for ages but using this English boat to carry our family mail was far easier and more reliable.

Caroline deejays now came out to the ship under the guise of visiting the Mi Amigo on an anorak boat trip and we mingled with parties of excited fans to make it look real. The boat would pull alongside the radioship and bundles of supplies would be thrown into eager waiting hands. Next would come a crew change and a quick sail round the Mi Amigo to keep the anoraks happy.

It was a dangerous business for the boat owners and it's sometimes easy to be complacent about the tenders but they took an extraordinary risk on our behalf. There was no glory in it for them and although the journeys out to the ship were pretty grim at times, they were a necessary evil; either they were endured or you did not work for Caroline.

Anorak conventions were a normal part of shore leave, many taking place in Holland, and one such event took me to Noordwijkerhout in the south of Holland, a place famous for its bulb fields. I flew out to Schipol on the Friday afternoon and stayed with Frank van de Mast, my Radio Mi Amigo colleague.

This was my first Dutch radio day and I was surprised and flattered to find that Stuart Russell was pretty popular with the Caroline listeners. Signing so many autographs was a new experience but I got used to it eventually and warmed to the whole procedure.

Walking into the conference hall, I felt a little overwhelmed at the number of people who had gathered to talk about offshore radio, mostly Radio Caroline and Mi Amigo. So many radio people to whom I had listened over the years were milling around; it made me feel like the ultimate anorak. Tony Allan made a beeline for me and joined me in a corner where I found myself explaining the pros and cons of living at sea to a group of young fans and would-be deejays. I felt on safe territory here as Tony could not pull rank and go on the attack. Next to find me was my Dutch friend from the ship, Herman de Graaf.

He was a fair bit older than most of us and must have been at least thirty! He had a big ginger moustache of which he was very proud, but that led some to refer to him as the 'Village Person.' I liked Herman and we walked around the hall clutching our drinks. A boy called Sebastian from Amsterdam was keen to be a deejay on Radio Mi Amigo and was talking excitedly in Dutch to Herman, who showed an interest but had no authority other than to utter the usual mantra to hopeful deejays, which included sending a tape to the office in Spain. I knew how the boy felt, for this burning desire to broadcast from the Mi Amigo is the same feeling I had as I grew up and it was just pure luck that saw me realise my dream. Maybe this fellow would have the same luck in the future.

The tannoy suddenly burst in to life, jolting me out of my day dreaming. It announced, 'Radio Caroline and Radio Mi Amigo deejays to the stage please'. This was the bit I was dreading, as I suffered from a morbid fear of crowds and talking in public.

I was reminded of school and my enforced participation in so many school plays. Naturally, they involved remembering lines, so that was far worse than anything today held. I remembered the dry mouth on the school stage as my lines approached, the nervous shaking of my entire body and firing the lines out at breakneck speed, as though my life depended on it.

One particular play in which I appeared was *The Government Inspector*, a St Edmund's School production which required several boys from the prep school to play the children. Unfortunately, I was cast as *Marya*, the daughter of the government inspector, which involved hugging and kissing my sixteen year old male mother. Jacob Rawlings minor was not a particularly good looking fellow and looked far more stupid than I did in drag. Opening night arrived, with my mother and father in attendance. I was ten and scared rigid that my father would go mad seeing me in girl's clothing. I was consumed with worry as his attitude to 'that sort of thing' was very draconian. Nothing was said, fortunately, and the performances seemed to go well.

This time, my stage appearance was nothing by comparison and I was seated alongside some seasoned old professionals. Graham Gill, a trouper from Radio North Sea International and the Caroline days when she was off the Dutch coast, Andy Archer who had been with Caroline for many years along with other offshore stations. Tony Allan was there, along with Ferry Eden and Herman de Graaf from Radio Mi Amigo.

I was enjoying the superstar status and the questions came thick and fast; how did this happen, how did that happen, what happens when the police come alongside our ship? And so on, and so on. My nerves soon evaporated and I was rolling around with delight on stage in front of the adoring fans who applauded almost every word.

I flew back to England late that night and my mother picked me up at the airport. We were soon heading back to Kent through the late Saturday night traffic.

I was due in London on the following Monday for a meeting, as I was scheduled to return to the Mi Amigo later in the week.

I had met the boss, Ronan, several times by now, but only for short periods and had not really got to know him very well. Now I had been summoned to see him in London before going back to sea. He has been described as many things over the years from hero to villain and probably everything in between, but I have always had a huge admiration for him. I think he liked Stuart Russell and he always seemed pleased when we had briefly met before.

This occasion was my first visit to the *Casserole*, his preferred restaurant on the King's Road in London. I arrived a little late and entered a room bustling with chatter. Ronan was seated alone in one corner talking to a waiter, no meal in evidence yet. I walked over to him.

'Baby, sit down', he said, introducing me to the waiter; his manners in this respect were always impeccable.

'Meet Nigel, he's one of my best!' I was flattered, but wondered what the waiter thought he meant.

Smiling, the waiter then handed a menu to each of us in turn. Ronan asked about my mother. I told him she was well and that I would say hello on his behalf. The conversation turned to the boat and how I felt about the future of Caroline. I told him we all had a good feeling out on the ship, we got on well and things looked good. Of course, he had a better idea than I did about the state of play. I knew he'd had a secret meeting with Sylvain Tack, the boss of Radio Mi Amigo, only a few weeks before. But I believed I was only here at his request for an informal chat and in my early Caroline days, I was not equipped to discuss much of the politics.

It was now that I discovered the real reason for being summoned to London. Ronan wanted me to go to Holland the next day to collect the *K-Tel* tape. This was a commercial that ran on Radio Mi Amigo every hour before the news throughout the day but it was Ronan's deal and it paid a lot of money. *K-Tel* produced compilation albums and various household items; each advertisement would run for several weeks until a new one arrived from Holland, closely guarded by the Caroline individual who had been sent to collect it. I did the run on many occasions and each trip was an escapade in itself. Hence, I sat in the King's Road learning how important it was to the company that the run was made in total secrecy. I could manage this, I thought, even though it was totally cloak and dagger. That was the way of the station and accomplishing the task should not be too difficult.

We ordered our food and I listened to the benefits of a world with plenty of *Loving Awareness*. This was a concept Ronan was keen to propagate through the radio station. It was fundamentally being nice to each other and doing to others the things you would expect from them. New Testament stuff indeed, and I loved it. He also wanted us to talk about it on the air, and that I found difficult. Some deejays managed to convey the idea, while others sounded embarrassed and insincere. So in the main, I steered clear of that facet of LA, as it was known. I only played the pre-recorded promotions.

As more drinks arrived, water for Ronan, wine for me, I made my apologies and headed for the toilets. When I got back to our table, Ronan was in full conversation. Several people were standing around him and they seemed quite content to let him do all the talking. They laughed at his witticisms and anecdotes, and that gave him the self assurance to carry on, entertaining them with more of his ideas and perceptions. I sat down amongst the ensemble feeling slightly embarrassed as our waiter arrived at the table to clear away our dishes. I smiled and said nothing as we finished our drinks.

Within minutes, Ronan announced that it was time to leave. We left the restaurant as more diners arrived and were shown to their tables.

I walked across the King's Road with Ronan and we went inside his flat where the search for cash got underway. Twenty pounds here, thirty pounds there; it seemed to be scattered in small amounts all over the place. Eventually, the total sum required was discovered and I left with seventy-five pounds for a return flight to Schipol airport in Amsterdam. My mission to collect the new commercial was underway and I headed off into the night in mum's car, the new little red mini that was to prove such an essential part of so many of my Caroline exploits.

CHAPTER 8

It was an early start in the morning, with the train to London Victoria and the bus across to Heathrow airport. The flight to Schipol in Amsterdam was without incident, although I was a little merry from the wine I had drunk on the plane to acquire a little Dutch courage. The rules, in true James Bond mode, required me to carry a copy of the *Herald Tribune* newspaper and wait in the cafeteria nearest the main exit. I sat with the paper open, clearly showing the front page and hoped nobody else was doing the same thing, by chance, with an identical paper. Within a few minutes, a man came over and glanced at me in a rather blasé manner and moved on. I watched as he circled the small eatery and smiled to myself as he came back for another look. I think I had him at a disadvantage on this occasion. 'Stuart? Stuart Russell?' he inquired. I stood up. 'Yes sir,' I replied. 'Ah, thank goodness,' came the reply. 'I've been waiting for about an hour, I thought I'd missed you.' He had been given the wrong time of my arrival.

'Let's order some coffee,' he suggested, 'You can put it on your expense account, I expect.' My eyes opened wide and a big smirk spread across my face. But I was, as far as he was concerned, a company man and must not let the organisation look bad, especially to an advertiser.

'Of course, let me order.' Hell, how do I pay for this? I furiously thought for ways out, but none came. I fiddled around in my pockets for the few guilders that I still had in change from the plane and I returned to the table with the coffee. 'Just one?' he inquired. 'Oh yes, I had a couple of cups whilst waiting here, that's enough,' I lied. He drank the coffee hurriedly whilst making polite conversation, and on replacing the cup in the saucer, he reached inside his coat pocket and pulled out a small package. This was the *K-Tel* commercial on a small reel of tape, so imperative to the station. 'Good luck, Stuart,' he said, standing to leave. I sat and watched him depart through the milling crowds, heads gawping up at arrival and departure screens. My mission was accomplished and I could go home.

I got a lift home from Gatwick from my mother, who met me at the airport. She asked me about the trip, pleased that I had not got myself into any trouble with the authorities. She was beginning to learn the oddities of this organisation and took it in good spirit, including all the extra driving she now had to do. For my part, it was good to have a driver, although a statement like that would never pass my lips in front of her.

The acquired tape came with me to the ship and was on the air within minutes of my arrival. I had come out to the Mi Amigo from Calais on this occasion, and again, the journey had been without mishap, albeit long. We had a good crew on the ship this time and even the imminent arrival of Tony Allan and his eccentricities would not deter me from enjoying my time on board.

The weather was getting better and the summer promised to be a good one. We were soon busy on deck during time off from the radio, painting, scraping and doing some general maintenance. Otto was our young Belgian sailor and he was always caked in paint, tar or diesel. His waking hours usually involved half-hearted repairs of some sort around the ship.

We had lost our main crew due to shortage of money and were without an official captain. Peter Chicago took on that role and other duties were shared between the team on board at the time. This involved the ship's duties and the all important cooking. Fortunately, we were soon to be relieved of this latter chore when a Dutch cook named Kees Borrell arrived on board.

Kees was a real jack-the-lad who would speak his mind in broken English at every opportunity. He had a shock of wild blond hair and a bullish but friendly nature. Women were his only thought for much of the time and miles out to sea, there was little he could do to alleviate the lack of the opposite sex. For him, and most of the other crewmembers, salvation arrived on the tender in the form of girlie magazines, which were ferreted away to various cabins below, where they would be scanned for any potential sexy pictures.

The popular Belgian music magazine, *Joepie*, was owned by Radio Mi Amigo boss, Sylvain Tack, who was now based in Spain with his radio team. Connections between the radio station and the magazine were tenuous and publishing articles about the Mi Amigo and the station's programme schedules seemed, for a while at least, to be tolerated by the authorities.

One particular month, the magazine arrived on the ship and included a poll of top deejays in Holland and Belgium. I have no idea how it came about, but to my amazement, the top three presenters on the European continent were Lex Harding, Stuart Russell and Stephen Bishop, who went on to become Johnny Lewis in later years. I had made it to number two! Lex Harding had been with Radio Veronica on the ship, *Norderney*, which had ceased broadcasting several years earlier when the Dutch

Marine Offences Act became law, outlawing the offshore stations. Lex was still with Radio Veronica but now involved in their new legal shore- based venture.

I gave my copy of *Joepie* to Ronan, who seemed very pleased that the station still had such impact. Sadly, I never saw that copy of the magazine again. However, a year later, another poll still put me in the top five, so I remained quietly pleased.

A new tender usually meant fresh supplies and that meant alcohol and cigarettes. There was always a fair chance these luxuries had long run out, so we were euphoric when there was a sudden abundance of goodies. I was always so pleased when Samantha appeared on the tender; my mood was instantly lifted when I saw her on the deck of the visiting boat. Her manner and style were her own and although she got so much wrong, mispronounced many names and forgot things, it worked and she was a genius on the air, as far as I was concerned.

We ate well one particular night at dinner and drank a lot of wine. We'd all had a good deal more to drink by late evening and Samantha was due on the air at nine o'clock. She left the messroom just before her show started, whilst I stayed upstairs drinking with the crew.

After a while, several people retired for the night and I went into the galley to make a sandwich. I jumped several steps at a time down the stairs, went into the storeroom at the bottom, grabbed some more wine and headed for the studio where Samantha was well into her programme.

As with the majority of the people onboard, Samantha loved to drink and thought nothing of going on the air a little intoxicated. I was in the studio with her and Marc Jacobs from Radio Mi Amigo. The show was fun and we laughed and continued to drink as the music blasted from the speakers. As the laughter continued between the songs, Marc had grabbed Samantha's breasts while the microphone was open and she commented, almost matter-of-factly, 'Stop touching my tits!' I went straight into shock and gasped for breath in between frantic schoolboy giggles.

It became infectious and took a good few minutes before the music restarted; there were no computers to take charge and no compact disc machines to start. This was vinyl territory and if nothing was prepared, any manic laughter or loss of control would always overcome attempts to cue up a track on a record. But Samantha was soon back in charge, and the show continued with little interruption.

Alcohol was my downfall on several occasions on the ship and unfortunately, sometimes whilst I was on the air. Trying to pronounce the name of bands such as *Renaissance* would give the game away at anytime. On one shameful occasion, I spent three days unconscious in my bunk after drinking a large bottle of vodka; not a clever move on my part and one which put me off alcohol for a good length of time.

I was to leave the ship and return to France again within the week. Two presenters had arrived from America and the London office team were keen to get them on the air.

Arriving back in Calais, I was told that we had an apartment for the use of the deejays who were coming from or going to the ship. Using the key that had been left with the tender skipper, I made my way across town. Our new resting place was in a rather upmarket block just outside the town centre, and I made my way up to our floor with a degree of embarrassment.

I was dirty, stank of fish and my jeans had been ripped whilst at sea. Due to the suddenness of my departure from the Mi Amigo, I had not had time to change. Therefore, I appeared with a huge hole torn in one trouser leg, smelling to high heaven and carrying a cheap bag with some tatty belongings. Trying not to be seen was a difficult task, but eventually I made my way to the Caroline rooms. At least half a dozen people made what I believed to be derisive comments in French as I meandered past them.

I sank into a warm bath and wondered what this apartment was all about, as it seemed so out of character for our organisation. However, despite my uncertainty, I slept well and awoke at lunchtime next day. Making sure I had my meagre belongings intact, I quietly left the building.

Sadly, the apartment was not to survive for very long as a raid by French police resulted in the arrest and deportation of Una. We may have got away with it for longer, save for the fact that the local police chief lived in the same building and word soon spread as to our activities. The affair effectively ended Una's association with Radio Caroline and we were all extremely sad to see her role finally come to an end.

CHAPTER 9

It was now late in the year and Roger Mathews and I had been on the ship for more than three months. Others had gone ashore, but no replacements had arrived and we found ourselves to be the only Caroline presenters onboard. For just the two of us, the long broadcasting hours were a problem and it became an arduous situation keeping the station on the air. The weather was bad and we saw no boats with English crew for months on end. A couple of tenders arrived from France with precious little fuel and food. The Radio Mi Amigo programme tapes were delivered less regularly and still nothing came from England; supplies were running short and we ate poorly and infrequently.

We went on the air for hours at a time, slept a little, and then went back on the air. Several of the Radio Mi Amigo deejays left the ship due to the deteriorating conditions on board and we found ourselves having to run the Mi Amigo tapes during the day as well. Even they ran out on several occasions. We were so tired and in the days before radio automation, somebody had to be in the studio at all times.

By chance, I found our salvation hiding in the record library. Due to earlier storm damage from water, there were no continuous music tapes to play, but I came across the 'Motown Story' in documentary form on six albums. This meant Roger and I could leave the studio for at least twenty minutes at a time and as it was a documentary, there were no gaps between the music tracks, just commentary. That sounded so much better than putting on our customary albums and we were satisfied that it was a justifiable, temporary solution to the staffing problem and we managed some well deserved breaks.

Except back on land, it was not viewed with much enthusiasm. The fact that Roger and I were stuck on the ship with no support seemed to mean little to those listening in the office, as I was to find out on my return to London, when I was severely reprimanded for the Motown idea.

Never did we mention on the air the worsening conditions onboard or the fact we were tired and below par all the time. I like to think we were consummate performers in this rite and I was proud of our feat. The office staff were not top of my list of favourite people for many a month.

The weather remained foul and the Mi Amigo seemed to be forever lying sideways into the sea, against the waves; she rolled constantly which made life very difficult and sleep impossible. We hardly felt like eating our meagre rations and struggled to get through each day. But it was to get worse.

We were due one of the worst storms to hit Europe in many years. Watching the television weather forecast one evening in the messroom filled us with horror. Roger and I looked at each other across the table in incredulity as we listened to the weatherman talking about north-easterly gales with winds of plus 45 mph, gusting to 70mph or more at times. We knew the seas would be huge and there was nothing we could do about it, except await the inevitable.

It was the eleventh of November, nineteen seventy-eight, when the gales reached their peak. The East Coast was hit by fierce gales with unimaginably strong winds and rough seas. The Mi Amigo moaned under the strain of the storm; fortunately she had turned and now pointed steadfastly into the wind, facing the huge rolling waves that bore down on her.

We had pulled ourselves out to the end of the straining anchor chain and were being held in place by the anchor itself, gripping the seabed far below, the chain now taut and under intense pressure.

The Mi Amigo was not a big ship, only four hundred and fifty tonnes; she had not been inspected in dry-dock since she was in Holland in nineteen sixty-six for repairs following a beaching on the English coast. Later, she had been laid up in harbour for four years after nineteen sixty-eight, but no work had been done to her; in fact she had deteriorated significantly. We knew she had leaks in her hull since lying on her anchor chain whilst on a sandbank a few years earlier. These leaks were dealt with when they appeared by hammering cone-shaped pieces of wood into the holes and pouring cement around the wood. It worked, but was a dreadfully sub-standard means of keeping a ship afloat.

Our main fear that stormy night was for our anchor chain, as without it, we were at the mercy of the storm. We had no working engine and no crew onboard; just a handful of radio presenters totally inexperienced in situations such as this one. Roger and I roamed about the Mi Amigo gripping on for dear life as the ship took on angles no vessel should ever experience. The waves were immense and as we peered out of the messroom windows, we caught sight of broken stays from the mast, flapping around in the shrieking wind, fleetingly lit by the arc lamps on the bridge. We had gone off the air a little earlier due to electrical problems caused by water virtually covering the main insulator on the foredeck. We now plunged so deeply into the furious seas, it became impossible to broadcast.

The strain on the anchor chain was gargantuan and the only way of telling that we were still firmly anchored was our continued facing into the weather. The Mi Amigo's bow facing into the crashing waves meant we were still secured but if that changed and we went sideways to these massive seas, we would know the anchor chain had broken, and the chances were high we would end up on a sandbank where the ship would probably break up; that was our great fear.

We had a spare anchor to be dropped in such an emergency, but in weather such as this, it was something we would rather not contemplate.

I opened the starboard hatchway door onto the deck to see what was happening to our gas bottles and other equipment stored outside; there was nothing left. Everything that could be torn away had been and the noise from outside was unbearable. The sound of the wind curling around every piece of structure and the groaning of the ship was fearsome. Every few moments, walls of water came crashing down the deck having come from the bow burying itself deeply into a new trough. I wanted to go up to the bridge to listen to channel 16, the emergency band, but knew it was a dangerous mission out along the main deck that led to the upper aft area and up to the bridge. There were moments when it looked as if a dash could be made, but I knew if I told anyone else my plan, there would be trouble and I would be barred from going. I said nothing and prepared myself.

Climbing into my duffle coat, I pulled up the hood and held open the hatchway door, pushing it out against the howling wind. I waited whilst a large wave subsided and the water washed away along the deck. The spray flew in the air as forceful as miniature knives, biting into my face as I stepped out. The wind was strong enough to pull a human being from the deck and toss him into the swirling waters; it was as cold as an Arctic night and pitch black beyond the lights from our little ship. The noise was even more incredible once I was outside, it was tremendous, even deafening.

Slamming shut the doorway, I crouched down and made my way astern towards the bridge whilst the sea poured over the gunwales and onto the deck, before washing away again. The tyres that formally hung over the side as shock absorbers for tenders coming alongside had all been washed up and over and were now hanging on the deck-side of the ship.

Abruptly, I felt the Mi Amigo plunge down into the next trough between the giant waves. I fell backwards, such was the angle of the ship, and sprawled out on the deck as water poured down in torrents over the side. Within moments, the Mi Amigo was riding up the front of the next wave and I was thrown in the other direction. I grabbed the rail running along the side of the deck-housing and held on for all I was worth as the water pulled with all its potent force at my legs as it swept down the deck. I pulled myself along deck rail and managed to climb towards the small steps which led to the back deck. A seagull hovered level with me a few feet away over the sea, and seemed to catch my eye for a few seconds as if to ask, what the hell are you doing out here? Get inside as fast as you can, idiot!

I was at the bridge door and gave the handle a sharp twist and fell inside. My dear God, I'd made it and any thoughts of checking lights on distant buoys or listening to the emergency band left my mind as I lay exhausted on the floor, the Mi Amigo continuing to pitch at horrific angles into the sea. I stood up and held myself onto the wheel housing, straining to see down the length of the ship through the spray, as she continued to fight against the storm. From the bridge, it was difficult to see much through the spray, save for when the ship took another dive between the waves.

I felt trapped and unable to get back to the main body of the ship. The waves crashed over the Mi Amigo, sweeping up and into the bridge and I was petrified that the glass would be smashed in by the sheer force of the water. Hanging on to things for safety for any length of time was impossible as the motion of the ship pulled me in all directions; it was a long ten minutes later when I changed my mind, deciding to make a break for it.

As the ship rode up the next wave, I left the wheelhouse and clambered my way down the water-drenched ladder onto the small aft deck which was riding up and down like a fairground ride. If I let go of the superstructure, I would be thrown over the side and this was made even worse now as the storm grew in intensity. The arc lights from the bridge continued to shine out into the night highlighting the viciousness of the seas in the area around the ship.

I again struggled along the heaving deck and on nearing the doorway, looked out across the water. I was rooted to the spot as I saw a massive rogue wave approaching from the starboard side of the ship. This should not be there as we were still facing into the seas but it was there, huge and dark, lumbering in our direction, just a few hundred feet away from us. I was almost on my knees as I reached the midway part of the deck where the accommodation housing was positioned. The thunderous sound of the storm had left me rigid with fright and exhausted from my unnecessary expedition to the bridge.

I kicked the metal handle down with my foot, pulled the door open and clambered back inside the ship as she took the full force of this latest monster. The Mi Amigo started the slow roll to port as she reeled under the onslaught. Water poured in around the doorway and into the bathroom and messroom.

I heard crashing from the galley as the wave breached the hatchway from the deck and there was a thunderous crash from the messroom as the television came free from its stand and hit the floor, the tube exploding. The roll to port continued and I fell across the corridor and onto the opposite hatch; the angle became too steep to stay upright. Water continued to pour in and was now cascading down the stairway as I saw several faces staring upwards in terrified disbelief.

People had arrived at the foot of the stairs as the Mi Amigo continued to roll over into what could only be a plunge to the bottom of the icy North Sea.

I realised the ship might not be coming back from this one and waited for the watery onslaught; I prayed hard in what I thought would be the ship's last moments. Those below decks were not able to climb the stairs as the angle of the ship made it impossible and water flowed in torrents down to the lower level.

But unexpectedly, I was able to get my footing again as the ship started to level out once more, and very slowly, she came back onto an even keel. The Mi Amigo was still struggling in the storm, but for now, she had resisted this furious sideways assault from the elements and beaten the menacing wall of water.

An innate sense relief overwhelmed me and I cried uncontrollably, screaming, 'Thank you, God,' over and over again. Drenched from head to foot, I staggered into the messroom as Roger and the others made it to the top of the stairs.

The ship was now in an appalling state, inside and out and it was still to get a lot worse before it got better. I met Roger in the hallway; he was as white as a sheet and I shook uncontrollably with fright. Now, I prayed hard for the storm to cease, I could not cope with this nightmarish state of affairs anymore. None of us could face anymore terror.

With every reel of the ship, I expected the chain to give way and hung on for dear life as the Mi Amigo continued to take a hammering. Chairs in the messroom were upside down and anything not nailed in position was flying around with each crashing wave.

I ventured downstairs with some difficulty to the record library and found chaos; every record, bar none, was on the floor and out of its sleeve. Water streamed down from the hatchway above the studio equipment as I threw a pile of rags over the mixer in a vain attempt to prevent more damage. Roger appeared and we tried to minimise any more harm to our precious electrical apparatus. The hours through the night were long and wearisome, but most of all, frightening.

As daylight broke, the winds dropped a little and the seas eased somewhat, giving us a chance to regroup.

We learned that the storm had caused considerable damage on shore with Margate Pier being demolished in the carnage that had taken place. We had suffered extensively onboard but the anchor had held throughout the storm and that was the most important factor in our survival. The disarray around the ship could be cleaned up and dried out over time and we could continue to broadcast once repairs had been made. Our mast had survived the dramatic storm with only a few stays being torn away, showing just how well it had been constructed.

Unfortunately, repairs took rather longer than expected and it was many days before we got back on the air. The Mi Amigo had kept us safe; bigger vessels have gone down in seas far less severe than the ones we had suffered on that occasion. She was battered and old, but had proved herself a dear friend.

Roger and I had been on the ship for four months by now and we were very eager to go home, especially after such a rough ride, along with the lack of food, staff shortages and the dreadful storm.

Christmas Eve brought with it a tender from England with Brian Martin, Peter Chicago and a cook; we still could not go home but at last we had supplies and company.

We celebrated Christmas and the New Year, a little subdued to say the least, but very enjoyable nonetheless. We constantly scanned the horizon for boats coming our way, but time after time saw nothing; the days rolled on and on.

The Belgian tender appeared in January with supplies and a Dutch crew, but still nothing from England, apart from a message that said all efforts were being made to get people out to the Mi Amigo. I had really started to wonder if I'd ever get off the ship.

Eventually, almost a month later, rescue came and this latest journey home took us back to Brightlingsea, near Colchester in Essex and the good weather we now experienced made the prospect of seeing land even better. A few drinks in the Anchor Hotel on the jetty was far more civilised than the last horrendous months at sea. The staff at the Anchor very soon got used to seeing bedraggled deejays trundle up the pier after a three or four hour trip back from the North Sea; they were most welcoming on our arrival.

One particularly nerve-racking trip I made back from the ship a few months later went into Zeebrugge in Belgium. This had ended with a mad dash across a car park as the crew from the Mi Amigo left the tender one by one at five minute intervals; our luggage was taken off later. We threw ourselves into a waiting car and drove off at high speed with the sound of police sirens getting ever closer. On this occasion, fortunately, the local force did not manage to catch up as we headed off into the side streets. We pulled over and were told to leave the car, get lost for an hour and meet up again further along the road. I did not get my luggage back that day but it did appear on the Mi Amigo again a few weeks later.

A French tender, late in the year, took me into Boulogne at low tide, and I was told to walk under the jetty to a long metal ladder which led to the main road outside the harbour. As the tide was out, the walkways were about a foot deep in sludge towards the bottom of the ladder. As I stepped onto the bottom rung and took another step, the sludge pulled off my trainers and despite searching on my hands and knees in the filth and muck, I could not locate them. I became encrusted in the filthy, grey, smelly sludge and when I took the ferry back to England, I was wearing only socks on my feet, smelling to high heaven. Nobody would come near me on the journey, and who could blame them? When I climbed into mum's car outside the railway station in Dover, I had really had enough.

There are two things I regret about my time on Radio Caroline; the first being that I did not take as many photographs as I would have liked, and secondly, that I did not keep a diary, save for a few odd days here and there.

One entry I did keep started when a tour of duty came to an end and a tender arrived at the Mi Amigo.

Friday...Finally, the English tender arrived. Off went Roger Mathews, Brian Martin, Mi Amigo dj Ferry Eden, Chicago and me. On came James Ross, Mark Lawrence, a new cook and transmitter engineer Martin Fisher. Arrived home at 1.00am after three hours on the boat back to

England. Not a bad journey home.

Saturday...Brian, Chicago and I went to the Caroline Roadshow in Ipswich. (These were very popular rock music shows put on by deejays who did not work on the Mi Amigo, mainly Robb Eden, Robbie Day and Harvey the Rabbit) *Robbie Day came to my house and drove us to Ipswich in his car. Robb Eden and Simon Dee* (Simon being one of the very first Caroline presenters) *were also there. 750 people got in but at least 200 were locked out. Had meal with Robbie Day on way back home.*

Sunday...Got up at 5.00pm and went to pub with my sister.

Monday...Up early and off to Canterbury. Frank van de Mast rang this afternoon. I will go to Holland next week for a break.

Tuesday...Another Belgian tender is due to go to the ship today. Fingers crossed it goes well.

Wednesday...Phone Lyn (London office) *to see if there is any money.*

Thursday...Caroline Roadshow in Norwich tonight. Too far to go this time. Call from Herman de Graaf (Dutch dj) *today with all the gossip.*

Friday...Caroline Roadshow in Margate tonight. Roger Mathews is coming down later. Snowed very hard today and it's very icy tonight. Roadshow an absolute flop and only a few people turned up. Robbie is drunk and hiding from Simon Dee who wants to be paid but there is no money tonight. I am to drive Robbie's car home but the battery is flat. I tried to bump start it down a slope but then find out you can't do that with an automatic. (Simon Dee was once more at the roadshow as a special guest and meeting him was a great pleasure. I found him unassuming and polite and we had an interesting conversation about the early days of Radio Caroline. However, it did not matter to him that numbers were low at the roadshow; he wanted to be paid. In the absence of Robbie Day, who had booked Simon, I appeared to be his next Caroline contact. Of course, I had nothing to do with the roadshows or any monies made from them. But Simon was determined to get his cash and as I tried to sneak away, he spotted me and gave chase. I quickly fled and managed to shake him off in Margate high street. I heard no more of the incident, so assumed Simon was later paid. Sadly, he died in August, two thousand and nine at the age of seventy-four.)

Saturday...Went to see Lyn in London with Roger and managed to get £60!!! We are both very pissed off. But Lyn said Ronan should have more next week. Heard that one before! Got home about 3pm and Robbie Day turned up and we went back to London to get some commercial scripts. That boy is a real pain at times. Ran out of petrol so stayed at Robb Eden's place. Went to wine bar. Exhausted. I need sleep.

Sunday...In London all day. Eventually got gas which was difficult due to the petrol tanker driver's strike. Saw movie at the Odeon, Leicester Square. Home with Robbie. We got very drunk.

Monday...Went off delivering records to shops with Robbie, (his daytime job) *but he locked us out of the car in Maidstone. Took hours to get in again with an old coat-hanger. He is such a twat.*

Tuesday...Flight to Holland. BA, Flight BA 216. Must be at Heathrow by 13.30. Guess what? I missed the plane by just a few minutes. Went home again then used the ferry. Should have done that in the first place. Had a good sleep.

Wednesday...Arrived 0700 to more snow, Frank van de Mast there to meet me with car. Went to visit Stan Haag (Mi Amigo dj) *for the day. Marc Jacobs arrived in the afternoon. Had a few beers later.*

Thursday...Went to The Hague for some sightseeing. Thrilling stuff!!

Friday...Frank has his first programme on Hilversum 3 tonight. Late, 2-5am. He's now quit Radio Mi Amigo. He's done well I think, and he's pleased but he was nervous!

Saturday...Up late then off to Brugge to Mi Amigo Drive-In Show with Marc and Frank. Also there was Bart van Leeuwan and Peter van Dam (Dutch djs) *P. van Dam was pretty drunk. Otto the sailor was there too.*

Sunday... Saw film and had a meal in the Park Hotel with the guys.

Monday...I am writing this on the KLM flight back to London. It's 07.23. Have 200 fags and some wine. I'll give the wine to mum and take the fags to the ship. Looking forward to seeing new house. Hello Sittingbourne.

And that's where the entries end. My mother had moved house over that weekend and we left the Isle of Sheppey to start a new life on the mainland. Mum had little reason to return to the island, but my Caroline ventures would ensure that I visited the place umpteen more times.

CHAPTER 10

Lyn was our new girl in the London office. She was a friend of Una, who, after the French difficulties, was now keeping her head down. The call came from Lyn late one Sunday afternoon; I was going back to the ship again.

As usual, there was no time to say goodbye to my friends as I had to go to London that evening to collect some equipment and commercials for the ship, before setting off for the North Sea.

There had recently been a burst of police action around the eastern coast in England regarding Radio Caroline. Peter Chicago, our engineer, was arrested one morning coming ashore in Gorleston, near Great Yarmouth and after a spirited speech in court in defence of the radio station, he was fined £150 and given a month to pay.

Due to the increased activity of the authorities, it was decided to use French tenders again for a while. This was not good news as far as I was concerned, as it meant another really protracted journey from the continent to the Mi Amigo.

Predictably, there were more delays before getting out to the ship. I was the only English person going on this French boat, as two others had gone out a fortnight before from England. The police had been sniffing around at the time but fortunately, they had not apprehended any of our team.

I went to see the skipper in Boulogne late the next afternoon but he was reticent about the whole affair and threatened to pull out of the trip altogether. The sight of the 'Caroline cash' worked wonders on this occasion, and when waved under his nose, the trip was back on.

Waiting to go out to the ship was mind-numbingly boring and I had only the money for the tender; it was not for any personal distraction. With my limited resources, I checked into the Hotel Alexander and then headed off into town. I discovered, yet again, there was nothing more likely to induce gloom than being in a foreign country, not knowing anybody and having little money.

After my previous trips to the North Sea, I should have been used to the loneliness of the wait, but it was always difficult. My mind wandered as I strolled around the town and I found a park bench alongside an empty café and slumped down. A waiter ventured outside and I avoided eye contact in the hope that he would ignore me. It worked.

My thoughts drifted in and out of boats and school days and I soon found a catalogue of melancholy tales to occupy myself while the hubbub of the street with its noisy business quickly evaporated to the back of my mind.

I remembered my first night at St Edmund's School in Canterbury; that innocent pillow-fight with some boys in the dormitory. It helped us forget our homesickness and our silly giggling helped drown out the pitiful sobs of some of the other boys, painfully weeping for their mothers. Some of the boys were only eight years old, so it was a very harrowing time for a lot of the children at a school such as this one. I often reflected that our parents must have really hated us to put us through this nightmare.

There was no senior boy in charge of the dorm that evening. We took advantage and played around to ease the pain of homesickness. My pillow came down on Michael's head with a resounding thump and he tumbled backwards, laughing. The lights were out, but there was enough illumination on this early September night to see who we were hitting. Adam joined in from the other side of the dormitory and he hobbled across the cold wooden floor in his pyjamas and bare feet, swinging his pillow in the air. I ducked under my bed as he came for me, and slid out on the opposite side. I jumped up waving my pillow in the air whilst beckoning to my assailants to come and get me.

It was at this very moment that the dorm door flew open and the light switches were banged on with a heavy hand. Mr. Trevis, master-on-duty, had arrived in the room having obviously heard some commotion. We froze instantly and all three of us looked over to the door. I felt my stomach lurch and I knew we'd be in trouble.

It seemed like an eternity before the man spoke, his face now taking on the look of executioner as he walked into the room and leant on an upright piano which stood against the wall by the main door; he removed some music, placed it on top of the instrument and lowered the lid quietly.

There were twelve boys in my dormitory, and each of them not involved in the pillow-fight lay still, their eyes peering above the blankets at the unfolding drama.

Mr. Trevis still did not speak but he looked at each of us in turn, then at his feet whilst shaking his head, his jowls wobbling to and fro; he then caught our glance. This man appeared well trained in the art of scaremongering and I shivered with fright as it dawned on me a mere telling off was probably not on the cards. Mr. Trevis was a stocky man, with short, well groomed hair. His dark grey suit seemed a tight fit, suggesting he had put on considerable weight during the school holidays.

He turned to us, 'Gentlemen', he said in a low, passive voice. 'It seems to me that you have no respect for the other boys here trying to rest their weary bodies.' He raised his voice a little and continued. 'Sleep is a very important part of your schooling, for without it, you will not be able to concentrate on your work or perform in any school activity.' He paused, breathing out heavily and rubbing his hands as he persevered with his denunciation of our activities. 'You are depriving these boys of their sleep. This is blatantly unfair to them, and now, gentlemen, to me. Put on your dressings gowns.' He moved to the centre of the room. 'Get out!' He pointed to us and then at the door; we walked out of the dormitory as he bellowed again at us. 'And look lively!' I had no idea of the trauma that lay ahead. The three of us waited for Mr. Trevis as he ordered the remaining boys to behave and then turned out the lights. We followed him through Matron's office, past the hobby-room and into the corridor which led to the library and one of the junior form rooms. He stopped us outside his office door and ushered Michael inside.

'Wait please, gentlemen,' he said to Adam and me, reverting to the low, calm utterances of earlier. I felt a little easier now; maybe it was just a telling off we were to get after all.

Michael went into the study and we stood outside, fidgeting nervously for a minute or so. A barely audible conversation came from within the room and I listened for a raised voice from Mr. Trevis to signify trouble, but heard none. Suddenly, there was a sound like a muffled bullet hitting a target. Mr. Trevis was beating the boy who at that moment let out the most piercing scream I had ever heard. I thought Michael would come out of the room now, but there were three more strikes still to come.

My thoughts for this boy soon disintegrated into anxiety for my own safety. When Michael did come out moments later, there were tears streaming down his face and he held his bottom, hardly able to draw breath. He hobbled painfully to the far wall and slid down to the floor, sobbing profusely.

I had no time to think before being pulled into the study by Mr. Trevis as he grabbed the lapels of my oversized dressing-gown. 'You don't fight when I'm around!' he barked sharply. 'We were only playing, sir, I'm sorry,' I squeaked, hardly able to talk. I wrestled the man as he tried to pin me down, but it had no effect and I was forced to lean over the back of a sturdy wooden chair.

'Grip the sides,' said the brute as he lifted my dressing-gown up and out of the way, before stepping back in order to supply more energy to his swing with the slipper. It came down hard on my backside, protected now only by my skimpy pyjamas bottoms.

I had never experienced pain like this before. My whole body went into convulsions as I screamed out at the top of my voice and stood up, only to be forced down again with a firm hand on the back of my neck for the second whack.

For Heaven's sake, what was going on? What was this man doing to me? The pain was unbearable and my legs gave way as I crumpled to the floor. 'Stand up!' came the order, and I struggled to my feet as Mr. Trevis pushed me over the chair again to administer two more wallops.

Adam was the bravest of all and not a sound left his mouth as the slipper crashed down on him. Not until he came out of the room did his face crack and the weeping take effect.

All three of us were sent back to the dorm blubbing and in a state of shock. There was nothing we could do about it and I felt trapped in a world of horror and torture, fraught with danger at every turn.

I tried to catch my breath as I walked the dimly lit corridors on the journey back to my little bed which would become a haven of safety, at least for a while.

We had each been beaten four times and in the morning we could see the bruising caused by the torment of a few hours earlier. I thought my parents would have something to say about it, but no; it was character building according to my father. My mother dutifully agreed.

At St. Edmund's School, there was a system of points available which could result in a beating. Running in the corridor, dirty shoes, answering back or any number of minor offences would get the perpetrator one 'B order mark'. Accumulate three of these and you would get an 'A order mark', resulting automatically in a thrashing. These beatings continued regularly during my years at the school. One particularly bad week earned me four whackings, two of which were with the cane, for crimes that these days would not warrant a second glance.

The most sadistic of masters was a man called Johnny Briggs. It was his first teaching post and he arrived at St. Edmund's in my second year at the school. He and I had a dangerous relationship and I believed most beatings were handed out to me just to please his sadistic tendencies. I was punished by this man more times than I was by all the other teaching staff put together. In those early days at school, I lived in fear of my safety when around this dangerous man. Several years later, he served a prison sentence for inappropriate behaviour with several boys in his care.

My piano teacher and head of music at the school, Mr. Brough, was a welcome sight when on duty. This duty involved being around at bedtime and if we were lucky, a story before lights out. Mr. Brough made himself doubly popular with his special guessing game. Putting his hand in his pocket, he would gather up his loose change and jingle it between his hands. We would guess how much was there and the boy who guessed the nearest would keep the money. It could run into several pounds on the odd occasion, and that made the winner very popular on tuck-shop days.

There was always a hoot of joy emitted by the junior boys on seeing the school chaplain's name down as the master-on-duty. The Reverend Christopher Gill was a kindly soul with a sympathetic temperament. He wore a black clerical cloak fastened at the front with a large silver clasp and was known amongst the boys as Zorro. Divinity lessons with him were a blesséd relief after the hard graft of Latin, maths and other challenging subjects. As for the Latin, I found it fairly easy to translate into English, but from the mother tongue into Latin, that was always beyond me. I had help from another boy, an older organist friend, Richard Kelsey, but in return I would have to hand over half my weekly pocket money.

The chaplain would invite us to his house across the road for tea if we were not afforded an exeat from school on a Sunday. These special days were eagerly anticipated, as his wife always showered us with the affection we lacked in school. And there was so much food; it was soon gulped down.

Not surprisingly, with my attitude to all things in school life, I was to eventually rub the chaplain up the wrong way, although it was a difficult thing to do to. One afternoon, he was refereeing a school football match, when I was kicked hard in the shins. Turning on the perpetrator, I kicked him back and issued a long list of expletives in full earshot of the chaplain. My outburst offended him to the extent that I was told to report to him after the match. Four of the slipper followed and I became the only boy ever to have been beaten by the school chaplain.

In the senior school, corporal punishment took on a strange twist with the older prefects, monitors as we called them, able to beat the younger boys; a handful of eighteen year old senior boys ruled in grandeur over the newly arrived fourteen year olds. Fagging was still in operation and continued to be for a year or two more. However, things did get better with successive headmasters and corporal punishment, along with so many of the more rudimentary elements of school life, eventually ceased.

If I can thank the school for anything, it was my introduction to music; not the music I would get involved with on Caroline, but choral and organ music.

Singing in the school choir, visits to Canterbury Cathedral and taking music lessons, piano and organ, got me away from the harsh reality of the school system for a few hours a week.

A typical day in the prep school meant getting up as the harsh bell clanged robustly in Matron's hand whilst she toured the dorms around the junior block just after seven o'clock in the morning. A quick wash in the small bathroom outside the dorm was next, with a fifteen minute run to endure afterwards. Breakfast followed, shoe cleaning, chapel and then off to lessons for the day.

Luckily, music would come to my rescue on many an occasion, as choir practice and music lessons enabled me to miss out on some sports afternoons. But not always, and I was to suffer on the sports field many times. No matter how bad the weather, sport was seldom cancelled, and rainstorms, howling gales and snow became par for the course.

Rugby was particularly gruelling and along with football, formed the major part of Michaelmas and Easter terms. Summer brought with it cricket and only an improvement in the weather made it more bearable. Summer term took on a sinister side too and it soon became standard practice for some of the older boys to seek me out on cricket days. Deemed an easy victim, I suffered an assortment of assaults, including being thrown down from a tree on one occasion and stripped naked on several others. I was always determined to fight back but when the time came, found myself unable to make much headway. Protesting never got me anywhere and to have informed my housemaster would have certainly caused more trouble from my attackers and probably a good beating up too.

Boxing was compulsory, and something else at which I was useless. I spent more time avoiding the flailing fists of other boys than trying to fight back in any form.

In the summer months, we swam in the wonderful unheated pool. Naked as the day we were born, at least until we were thirteen and on the way to senior school. Very embarrassing for those who hit puberty early, as some boys in the prep school at around eleven or twelve were sporting certain amounts of early adulthood, much to their chagrin.

I attended choir practice five nights a week, plus the weekend rehearsals, and then it was an hour's prep with bed at around eight for those under eleven. It was an hour later for the rest of the time at prep school. We had five baths a week, with showers every afternoon after games.

It was the chapel organ that held my interest more than anything else. This huge machine which dominated the gallery at the west end was my reason d'être. I could sit and stare at it for hours knowing that I had to play it as soon as possible. But it was not as simple as that; piano lessons had to come first and I started immediately and studied hard. The organ followed within a couple of years, as by then, at the age of twelve, I had been appointed organist at my local church, St. Peter's at Halfway, on Sheppey.

One term, a year or so later, a little band of my contemporaries joined me one night after lights out for a jaunt into the chapel; the game was to see who dared play the organ the loudest. Now when I say play, it was really just to lean on the keys and make a noise. Four of us ventured into the building sometime after midnight as the school slept. We crept past form room doors, down long, bleak, granite passageways and past the Headmaster's office. It was dark and scary and the old school seemed to creak and moan as we sauntered in a little line through the darkness towards the chapel.

I was the only one who had any experience on the organ so I slid upstairs into the organ loft and switched it on. Coming down again, I told the boys that the more stops they pulled out, the louder it would sound. The first boy went up into the loft and we heard a tiny squeak from the organ as he chose a very quiet stop, purely by chance. The rest of us sighed with disappointment as the second boy went up; the same thing happened, maybe a tiny bit louder. I was now becoming a little weary of this pussyfooting around and beckoned the other boys to come with me.

We went up together into the organ loft, high above the chapel, and I pulled out all the loud stops, including trumpets and horns. Then came my pièce de résistance; I leant on the keys with both arms. The noise was overwhelming as the organ gave a mighty roar and reverberated around the dark chapel. I looked around for reaction from my colleagues only to catch a glimpse of the last boy's back as he disappeared from view. They fled at top speed into the darkness below as I sat rooted to the spot in the wake of my incredibly brainless action. I couldn't move and froze to the bench awaiting the inevitable arrival of someone in authority.

It was a full minute or so before I had the nerve to slip silently away, safe in the knowledge that this foolishness had gone undiscovered. I can only imagine what my punishment would have been had I been discovered. I told the story to the organist in Canterbury Cathedral years later, and he thought it highly amusing.

My next sortie into impending adversity came towards the end of the next summer term when I found myself the centre of attention for all the wrong reasons. On this occasion, I left myself wide open to ridicule and I paid for it profoundly.

I lay in bed one cold night in the latter days of prep school; my thirteenth birthday being just days away. Being unable to sleep, I was waiting for the chimes to strike from the school clock on the main building. Nine...ten...eleven...twelve; seven hours until breakfast. Then after another eternity, a single dong; one o'clock had arrived with six hours to go. Sleep continued to evade me.

'Nigel?' came a cautious voice from Sean in the next bed. 'What?' I whispered back, turning onto my front to converse with more ease.

'Let me have a look at your new Tintin comics.' I could not sleep, so I thought there was no harm. 'Come on, then,' I replied. Sean had to come to me because I had the torch. He crouched down and slid across the gap between the beds, climbing in with me. We talked in hushed voices under the blankets and I switched on my torch, pulling the comics from beneath the pillow. We were great Tintin fans and laughed quietly at the stories.

Sean was from Tunbridge Wells and had been a day-boy in his first year, travelling with his father each day to school. It became a little more complex when his father changed jobs, so Sean became a boarder. He was a slender boy with blond hair and a big smile, but not given to making friends easily. He appeared aloof and rather callous at times and would be sent to 'Coventry' on many occasions each term. He was not a particularly well liked boy for the most part, and his insensitive attitude to other boys never seemed to diminish, whatever the occasion. However, he was a chapel chorister and would come with me to the organ loft when I played for services and we got on well.

It was only ten minutes or so later when my bed was suddenly lit up in the glare of a bright torch from the other side of the dorm. 'What's going on there? was barked in our direction. I had been giggling too loudly and had been heard. Sean and I stared at each other in the ghostly radiance of the torch and to my dismay, the dorm monitor got out of bed and switched on the main lights.

Sean slid out of my bed, and back to his own, as the whole dormitory looked on in the silence that enveloped the room. 'I'll deal with you two in the morning, now go to sleep, filthy little perverts.' That was the only commentary I was to receive that night. There was a lot of tutting and muttering from the other boys before the dorm monitor bellowed at them. 'Shut up, and go to sleep. It has nothing to do with you!'

I lay in bed, anxiously trying to come up with justifications, but there were none. Talking or reading after lights out was meticulously prohibited, but even worse, it seemed everyone thought we were doing a lot more. We had no idea what would happen the following morning and I whispered to Sean for reassurance; none was forthcoming.

Next morning, we were told by the dorm monitor that we were to be reported for unacceptable behaviour. I queried this observation and was told to go about my business; he told us he would be reporting the matter to our housemaster before breakfast.

Boys started making jokes within minutes of waking, concerning our alleged overnight activities. Shouts went out to warn others that I was dangerous and would rape anyone on the spot. I strenuously denied the story to anyone who would listen, repeating over and over again that Sean and I were only reading comics; not a soul would believe me.

They ran towards us in the school cloisters, shouting abuse. 'Homos,' they bellowed, 'Poofs, faggots,' and so many more accusations. I had never experienced cruelness like this before and had no idea how to deal with it.

The comic reading actuality was far too lacklustre for a school full of spiteful, teenage boys and so the story spread that I had been caught having sex. I could not believe that we were to be reported for something that had not taken place.

I was on duty in the chapel that morning to play the organ at both junior and senior school services. I also knew the events of the night before would have spread like wildfire through the school, so I made excuses to steer clear of breakfast, blaming an upset stomach. I went to the organ loft early to circumvent the senior boys coming into chapel for the eight-thirty service. The morning sun poured through the lofty windows, shining into the choir aisles and striking the golden cross on the altar.

I sat alone in the cool stillness, trembling with trepidation at possible outcomes and did not notice the little red light flashing to signify the start of the choir procession taking place far below. The choir processed up the Nave and into their places in silence; I should have been playing some music. To add to my problems, I realised there might be trouble over this lapse in my concentration.

The first service over, I waited, this time with full concentration, for the red light to flash above the console that would announce the arrival of the choir procession for the junior school service. This second service had organ music to start the proceedings, albeit sombre to match my mood.

They were both very complex services to play and as my mind was still firmly on the previous night, I really had to concentrate, as never before.

I had planned to play a new piece of music that morning, something I had been working on for many weeks. But Mendelssohn's Prelude and Fugue, Number 2 in G major, would have to wait for another day; a day when I felt less distressed.

I knew from school tittle-tattle that the incident, of which I had been falsely accused, could result in expulsion and that made me even more apprehensive. To make matters worse, I noticed that the Headmaster was downstairs reading one of the lessons in the first service. I watched him from my vantage point high up in the loft and realised that he was probably contemplating what would happen to me in just a short while. I looked away and stared at my hymn book.

After the two services were over, I switched off the organ and gathered my schoolbooks, hoping I could head off to my form room for double English. But things were about to change for the worse; a boy clambered up the stairs into the organ loft and announced that my presence was required below. He said sternly, 'The Head wants you.'

My stomach churned and my head dropped down in absolute desperation at my impending fate.

'Now, so hurry.' said the boy in a low voice. This boy, whom I recognised but did not really know, was probably aware of the situation, as he looked extremely self-important whilst carrying out his directive.

I came downstairs and passed a number of senior boys collecting hymn books at back. I felt huge pangs of humiliation sweep across me and sheepishly walked out of chapel and across to the Head's office.

Sean was sitting outside, but we did not speak. I was feeling very irritated and wanted to blame him for this sorry business, but I knew I was as blameworthy as he, and would have to suffer the consequences.

'Have you been in yet?' I eventually asked Sean. 'No, he's not in there. His secretary says he will be a few minutes.'

'Does she know what it's about?' I ventured. 'I don't know,' was the answer, as Sean looked everywhere but at me. 'We were only looking at comics, for goodness sake,' I added, in a desperate, high-pitched squeal.

I paced up and down the short corridor that led to the front car park on one side and senior school on the other with the chapel entrance around the corner. I put my music and schoolbooks down on the bench outside the Head's office and sat next to Sean.

'You sir, inside!' I looked up to see the Headmaster appear and without pausing, he marched into his office. I sauntered slowly into the room behind the him as Sean sat rooted to the spot. I glanced back at him as I left the corridor; his eyes were wide open and staring blankly ahead. .

'Close the door, please,' came the order from the Headmaster. He was a tall, well-built man with a full head of dark hair, unkempt eyebrows and hairy nostrils. He was wearing his dark gown and academic hood as he always did for lessons, and this unplanned aggravation at the start of the day was obviously infuriating to him. He sat down at his desk as I stood against the heavy oak door, having closed it. Then the narrative began.

'Never before in my entire life have I heard such a sorry tale.' He leant forward, looking at me with total abhorrence. He continued, 'I have never come across a more immoral state of affairs in all my time at this school.' He ordered me closer to his desk and I cautiously shuffled towards him.

I wished he would just cut to the quick, get it over with, and let me know my punishment, but from his observations so far, it appeared that I was already culpable. My mouth was dry and I felt sick. Please get on with it, I pleaded to myself.

'I had such high hopes for you. You are the envy of the musical fraternity here, for you play the organ in chapel at the age of thirteen. That is an accolade, an honour afforded to few boys your age, if any.' He raised his voice quite substantially and I squirmed at the sound of it. He stood up and walked around his desk.

'And you repay the school with this degenerate conduct. You have disappointed me on the very highest stratum. You have brought shame upon your house and upon your school. What have you to say?' The words rang out in my head with convulsive force.

The attack came as a severe shock, it was all too much and he now shouted at me with unbridled animosity. 'You are a reprehensible boy, a humiliation to the school. Your form, your masters and the entire school will feel extremely let down by your behaviour. Understand me well; the punishment must be rigorous for this unfortunate behaviour.'

He delivered the body blow within seconds; expulsion was probably the only option. I thought I would be physically sick at any moment and I felt my knees about to give. I could not talk my way out of this situation. No words came and I struggled to make sense of it all, totally unable to speak. Tears were welling up with increasing force and I knew it would not be long before I lost control.

I stood stock-still, the Head's words beginning to jumble up in my mind and I became unaware of anything else he said over the next several minutes.

I snapped back to reality as he finished his condemnation. 'This school is far bigger than any boy here, especially you two reprehensible nuisances. And you sir, nasty creature that you are, I am told it was only three days ago you were beaten for stealing!' It was true; I had unthinkingly pinched a b a r of chocolate from a boy's locker. I had admitted the theft and paid the boy back, but still received six of the cane from my housemaster. The odds of me getting away with this latest incident appeared to be losing ground very rapidly. 'Wait outside and send in the other boy.' I had to act before it was too late.

'Sir, nothing happened,' I pleaded, looking up and into his eyes.

'That is not what I am told by your housemaster.' He stared at me in silence, waiting for a reaction. All I could venture was, 'But nothing happened, sir. We were talking, just talking and reading comics, sir.' The Head said nothing and I knew I was wasting my time. He walked to the door and shouted across at me, pronouncing every word clearly, precisely and very slowly, 'Boys don't just talk whilst in the same bed. You are fully aware of that, and it takes only a modicum of intelligence to grasp the true state of this shameful affair.'

'I have done nothing wrong, sir!' I begged again, 'Please sir, don't!'

The second time was out of sheer desperation and quite inaudible. The Headmaster stood in front of me saying nothing more. I whispered through the streaming tears, 'You can't do this to me.'

He spoke once more, this time without shouting. 'I have never had a boy lie to me and escape punishment. Wait outside!' I turned to leave and performed the obligatory, 'Thank you, sir', and bowing my head, I went back into the corridor as Sean went into the office.

The game was up, I now realised it; a blameless act had ended up with probable expulsion and total humiliation. It was so unwarranted, as I had been doing harm to nobody and now faced the ultimate disgrace due to a single-minded Headmaster.

I sat on the hard bench in the corridor, my head in my hands, gulping for air between the quiet sulks that now overwhelmed me. After a minute or so, I gained control, took a deep breath and sat up properly. The Head's secretary came over to me and ruffled my hair, saying it would be alright. I was not so sure.

Sean reappeared after five minutes or so with the Headmaster alongside him; there was no chance of talking alone to my partner in crime. The Headmaster grabbed me by the shoulder and walked me back into the office.

'You are two very lucky boys,' he said calmly as he opened his desk and removed the cane. I swallowed hard; this whole business was astounding.

The punishment was to be a beating with six of the cane for both of us. All privileges were to be suspended with no movies, no television, no leave to go home and continued detention. We were to lose three precious Sunday exeats which meant whole weekends at school, virtually on our own. There was no form of appeal.

Notwithstanding my anticipation of a beating, the relief of non-expulsion seemed to lessen the fear of the pain to come, if only slightly.

I was told rigorous consequences would follow if there were anymore such activities, as this sort of behaviour would not be tolerated at the school by any boy. It would be expulsion next time, undoubtedly. I said I would heed the warning, for there was little point arguing with the Headmaster any further.

I bent over where I stood and was told to hold my knees tightly and not to stand up again until all six strokes had been delivered. The pain was excruciating and flowed through my small frame with every strike, the tears streaming down my face yet again. I opened my eyes, but the vision was too blurred to see anything. It felt like an eternity, and then it was over; I stood up, pulling my handkerchief from my trouser pocket.

The Head told me to leave. 'Thank you, sir,' I said, as the pain throbbed through my body and the tears continued to flow. I had to accept that the whole school, including the Headmaster, thought we had engaged in regrettable activities, and no amount of protestation would change that fact.

I had to get away and hide, so I went from the Head's office and back into the chapel where the organ loft gave me a little time to be on my own. But only for a few minutes as another boy arrived for practice and I had to leave.

Sean was receiving the same brutal treatment I had endured as I walked out of chapel and off into school.

It is an event that makes me baulk to this day, but after that episode, I made sure that when the lights in the dorm went out, I went to sleep.

Children are sadistic beasts, especially to each other, as I found out over the following weeks when the malicious jibes continued to increase in measure. But very little that happened later was as callous as the vicious beating from the Headmaster.

Nothing lasts forever, and eventually the school forgot about my embarrassing experience and life settled down once again.

Noisy Frenchmen across the road snapped me back from my thoughts and I looked up to see three or four men arguing quite strenuously. Two women with buggies stopped short and took their babies to the other side of the road. A couple had appeared looking for some al fresco coffee and a waiter had trundled out to their table. I thought his scruffy apron and trainers really showed this café off as a place to be avoided. I looked up and down the boulevard and decided it was time to move on.

Two other lads had arrived from England to join me on the journey to the ship and we left the next day for the Mi Amigo in heavy seas, and after a long, tedious, bumpy ride, we arrived at the ship some nine hours later.

The Mi Amigo had had little or no maintenance work done for years and was really starting to show her weak spots. The hull was heavy with seaweed and barnacles around the waterline, although it was assumed this addition to the ship helped keep her stable in bad weather. Somehow I doubted it, but it could not have done any harm. Nothing was repaired anymore and bit by bit, the ship continued to suffer. No spare parts arrived and there were no repairs to the generators; only infrequent oil and filter changes took place. The anchor chain was never checked and was likely to break at anytime in bad weather, despite warnings from those on the ship.

We had two Mann generators onboard which had been installed years earlier. They were real work horses, but needed servicing regularly. There was a smaller generator, a Henschel engine, which could keep us on the air, but with far lower power. We were always switching to this power supply when fuel ran low and cries of disappointment would escalate as some unfortunate deejay realised his programme would only be broadcast on a few kilowatts instead of much higher power.

Our tender pulled alongside the Mi Amigo in a heavy swell and the skipper had immense difficulty holding us steady as the seas pulled effortlessly on his boat. One second we were below the Mi Amigo's bulwarks and the next we were thrown way up above them.

This was not a fuel run, so we had only people, luggage, boxes of food and a few sundries to transfer, but it was to be a long process. When my turn came to climb aboard, I balanced on the side of the tender holding tightly to the cavorting wheelhouse.

'Jump!' I heard the word bellowed through the crashing of the waves and instinctively let go and threw myself at the Mi Amigo. Instead of landing on the deck of the ship and falling into the arms of the waiting crew, I hit the rubber fenders, sliding down the side and under the water between the two vessels. As the swell rose again under me, it pushed me up and above the tyres before the tender crashed against the side of the radioship. Frantic hands grabbed at my body as I hovered above the swirling foam.

It was all over in a flash and although drenched in the coldness of the North Sea, it wasn't until much later that I realised how lucky I had been as I hovered between drowning and being crushed between the two vessels.

CHAPTER 11

It wasn't long before I was in more trouble, but on this occasion, not life threatening. The problem occurred early one Sunday morning after another night of drinking. Everybody else who had been involved in the alcohol abuse had gone to bed and that left Peter Chicago and me alone in the messroom, draining the last of the alcohol and discussing a wealth of current affairs, an activity so enjoyed by Peter. In truth, I only half listened, and nodded occasionally as Peter spoke on a range of subjects as diverse as Nostradamus on the one hand to Hitler's foreign policies on the other.

The Dutch duty presenter had not arrived by six that morning and it was time for a pre-recorded religious programme to start. We found the necessary cassettes in the studio and dutifully started the tape at the allotted time. Sitting in the studio against the back wall, it soon became difficult not to sing along to the hymns, and so, putting in our own words, we bellowed over the Dutch singers. Sadly, alcohol had clouded our judgement, and Peter decided the listeners were missing out on this treat. We put on headphones, whacked on the microphone and started to sing at the tops of our voices. Our additional words contained neither bad language nor contentious remarks and made little sense.

Needless to say, within the hour, we had headed off to our respective cabins to sleep off the previous night's pursuit. I was awoken about four in the afternoon by the arrival of a tender from Belgium, bumping alongside the Mi Amigo. By the time I got up on deck the worst was over, but there had been big trouble and it lay with the day's early morning hymn singing.

Naturally enough, the company behind the programme were livid at the hijacking of their broadcast and a special boat had been sent out to the ship to remove those responsible.

The saving grace was Peter, for if I had been with anyone else that morning, we would have both been hauled off the ship, never to return. But removing Peter was a different matter and the whole running of the radio station would have suffered as he was the captain and chief engineer, equally important positions. I think God knew we meant no harm, but the event was never to be repeated. I got into some trouble with the Dutch staff onboard but I was a good boy after that appalling episode.

On this visit to the ship I had brought with me a cassette, recorded in my bedroom at home from the television; it was a commercial I really liked and I thought it would sound rather classy on the air. We played it twice a show on Caroline, making it sound as if we had international advertisers; this was never the case. The advert was for the drink Martini and it all became rather incongruous when we had a visit from London Weekend Television with Janet Street-Porter and a very seasick soundman. The advert was played as part of the television programme, suggesting we had several big advertisers. Little did they know I had recorded it from their own television station a few weeks earlier.

I was on the air when the television crew arrived at the Mi Amigo, but they would not come onboard as they had been warned not to do so by the British authorities. Legally, they had every right to come onto the ship, as long as they did not offer us any creature comforts, as stated in the *Marine Offences Act, 1967.*

Questions were shouted at us across the water as the small fishing boat tried to remain close enough to make contact. Janet Street-Porter used a megaphone to carry her voice across the deep, but it was still difficult to make out her comments. I had to keep running back to the studio as my records were ending, so when the programme was transmitted after editing, I kept disappearing and would then suddenly reappear on another part of the deck as if it were a scene from television's *Bewitched.* I was easy to spot though, as I wore a brightly coloured rugby shirt, a promise made to my mother so she could easily identify me when she viewed the show.

It was the first time I had been involved in publicity such as this and I was pretty excited at the prospect of becoming a television star overnight. The authorities were less than happy, as their stern warnings to LWT not to visit the ship had gone, in the main, unheeded. In their opinion, we should have received no publicity at all.

Radio Caroline had won that contest, thanks to London Weekend Television.

CHAPTER 12

The Mi Amigo had weathered many storms in her life, and was weakened a little more on each occasion. By now, there was no maintenance to either ship or equipment and each day became more and more difficult as we struggled to stay on the air.

Rumours were rife onboard regarding the Radio Mi Amigo organisation leaving Caroline and going it alone with their own ship. The Dutch crew had evidently been sworn to secrecy and would say nothing; this added to an already strained atmosphere on the ship.

Early one morning just after four o'clock, I was on the deck getting some fresh air, when I spotted our Belgian tender steaming towards us through a reasonably calm North Sea. It was an unexpected visit but none the less very welcome, as conditions onboard were dismal, with a shortage of food, water and diesel. Not to mention the fact that the Dutch crew were getting very irascible as they had been out at sea for several weeks and this was a long time for any Dutch crew.

But a bizarre thing happened this time, for the visiting boat stopped a couple of hundred yards from the Mi Amigo and drifted around us for a good hour or so. She then moved forward and was soon steaming alongside the radioship; we tied her up as we would have done on any other visit. But this time, no hoses were passed over for fuel or water and no supplies were taken onboard. The language was purely Dutch, no English was spoken and it was a struggle to make anything of the conversation. The speed of their speech was camouflage, thus hindering the English crew in their understanding of anything. Even our so-called Dutch radio colleagues now gave us the brush off and would not engage in dialogue.

After lengthy negotiations with the visiting crew in our messroom, the Dutch and Belgians left the Mi Amigo and clambered aboard the tender. They undid the ropes and slowly pulled away from us. Their boat then headed off in the direction of England and we racked our brains as to why. What could they be doing going to the east coast of the UK? But without warning, from about half a mile away, the boat turned and headed back towards the Mi Amigo at full speed. We called them on the radio, but to no avail. Some of us were lined up along the deck, watching in disbelief as their boat bore down on our ship. As it got closer, we started to disperse not knowing what to do; a collision seemed inevitable.

We were all shouting at each other in abject astonishment; several people climbed back inside the ship as others ran to the bridge and called the coastguard. Whilst this was going on, the tender, which by now was fairly close to us, suddenly slammed the engines into reverse and turned to starboard, thus avoiding a collision at the very last minute. They had possibly decided the damage to their boat could be fatal, whatever the damage caused to our ship. Perhaps the crew had been talked out of it by our former Dutch colleagues who had just left the Mi Amigo. Or maybe it was all done as a scare tactic.

But that was not to be the end of the nightmare, as within fifteen minutes, having reorganised themselves, they hovered at our bows with an oxyacetylene torch trying to get a burn on our anchor chain. Fortunately, they were thwarted by the movement of both vessels and no cutting took place.

Then totally out of the blue, we were more than pleased to see an Essex police boat speeding towards the scene, blue light flashing in the early morning haze. We cheered with all our might and ran up and down the deck waving to our rescuers. The Belgians saw them too and headed off towards the continent at full speed, the police boat in hot pursuit.

We were never to see the tender again nor have any contact with our former colleagues. Unknown to us at the time, they were almost ready to move onto their new radioship and certainly did not want any competition. It appears they were quite happy to destroy us and our ship in the process. But luck was with us and we survived to broadcast another day.

But for Radio Caroline's credibility, the episode looked calamitous as far as the authorities were concerned, and we appeared to be nothing more than pirate gangsters fighting it out on the high seas.

The nineteenth of January, nineteen seventy-nine, saw an emergency call from the Mi Amigo which was answered by the Thames coastguard. The ship had suffered more cruel weather, and had again taken on a lot of water.

The Harwich lifeboat was launched and five people, including Roger Mathews, Tony Allan and Tom Hardy were taken off the ship leaving the Mi Amigo to spend the next twelve hours lying abandoned, fifteen miles out in the cold, dark, wintry North Sea.

Emergency meetings were held in London and I attended one in Highgate. For the time being, we hoped the ship's pumps were coping with the situation. Provisions were gathered and a small crew set out for the Mi Amigo, not knowing whether she would still be at anchor or on the bottom of the North Sea.

One of our men, Gareth, managed to get out to the Mi Amigo on his fishing boat along with Peter Chicago. They found the ship wallowing in a heavy swell and listing heavily. Chicago leapt aboard as the tender made a close pass, shouting, 'Goodbye, I'll be fine!' in answer to pleas not to remain onboard. He subsequently spent a night alone on the North Sea, desperately trying to keep the ship afloat.

The next morning, another boat arrived alongside the Mi Amigo. Skippered by Terry, our regular tender drew alongside the wounded radioship. She was still listing badly but remained afloat with Chicago still alone onboard. This time, new pumps, along with cement and other supplies were being readied for a full-on rescue effort. Below decks, the water was knee high in places and the pumps were put to work with an almighty task ahead of them.

Our intrepid band, including Roger Mathews and Tony Allan, got to work immediately and with a lot of perseverance and determination, things were repaired and many problems resolved. But Radio Caroline was still off the air with substantial generator problems whilst the Radio Mi Amigo organisation, with their new radioship, readied themselves for broadcast.

We were all down in the dumps at the situation but at least our ship had been saved and in time, could broadcast again.

The Caroline Roadshows continued as usual up and down the east coast with Robb Eden and the team, but without any on air publicity, audiences were very low.

Our Caroline team in Holland were now on the lookout for a new partner to take over the daytime broadcasting hours. I spent some time onboard after we went off the air whilst some presenters went in search of work on the local radio circuit. The main port of call for some was the Voice of Peace, but I decided to stay with the Caroline organisation and help get the station back on the air.

The storm that had so damaged the Mi Amigo had also washed a large barge ashore on Margate beach. The owners lost interest in it soon afterwards and sold it to a man from Margate, who was a keen Caroline listener. He was known locally as 'Earthquake Peter'. A slightly eccentric man with controversial views on earthquakes and their effect on mankind was destined to come to the rescue of Radio Caroline.

Our man Robb Eden had several meetings with the earthquake 'expert' and it was agreed that Caroline would broadcast his views on how earthquakes affect the planet. He would pay for ten tons of fuel for the Mi Amigo, taken to the ship on his newly acquired barge.

The long and demanding task then got underway to dig a channel to the sea so that the barge could be refloated. Earthquake Peter and many of the Caroline team spent long hours undertaking this back-breaking task. Repairs to the barge were an extra challenge to make her seaworthy again for the trip to the Mi Amigo.

This journey was a time consuming and difficult exploit in itself with our barge sailing too far north and getting perilously lost. Directions were finally acquired from a passing ferry and our barge turned south. Eventually, after nearly giving up and making for the nearest land, the Mi Amigo was located.

It had been a very difficult time for the radio station, as not being on the air was losing us precious revenue and listeners were going elsewhere. There was still much work to do before any sound came from Radio Caroline's transmitters and all efforts went towards this end.

Tony Allan was to reopen the station on the fifteenth of April, nineteen seventy-nine and I really wanted to be out at sea but had to be on land helping with the supplies and tenders. When Caroline finally took to the air, the first programme was a dream come true, as so many listeners and staff had thought she would never make it back again. I knew the authorities were not celebrating on that day.

Tony was his usual candid self on the air and his thanks and thoughts went out to all those involved in Caroline's triumphant return.

We had a new Belgian station on the air during the daytime, now using the Radio Caroline name. This station came on the air a couple of hours after Tony's welcome back show. Tony, however, remained with Caroline for only a few months more before heading off to Ireland; he never returned to the Mi Amigo.

One or two former presenters from Radio Mi Amigo reappeared, along with some new names and we headed into what would be the radioship's last summer at sea. The Conservative party had swept to power in the UK in May of the same year and we thought that after all the problems we had endured under the previous administration, it would be plain sailing from now on. But, how wrong could we have been, as time would tell.

CHAPTER 13

Both English and Dutch services were now called Radio Caroline. The Dutch service came under the control of Danny Vuylsteke, a short, rather dumpy Belgian businessman who took to his new role with a certain amount of panache. He drove a Porsche and frequently dined out in expensive restaurants.

A business-like interest in me was forthcoming as I appeared to be a rather undemanding person with whom to deal. I was willing to help him out as he grappled with his new role and became his English assistant and the go-between twixt him and Ronan whilst Freddie Bolland and Ben Bode, two Dutchmen, were our link to Holland. I now spent all my shore leaves in Belgium and Holland, going home to England very infrequently.

It was interesting to see how advertisers squirmed and tried to wriggle out of paying their bills when Danny and I arrived; heated arguments would go on late into the night and if a deal was not reached, we would go back in the morning. There were, however, some rock solid advertisers who paid on time, and quite well too. These were the mainstay of the station's income and oddly, included several chicken restaurants, hence the abundance of frozen chickens on the ship at the time.

Danny would pay me some income when I worked with him, but I had to present the Caroline Roadshow in Belgium to earn this money. We visited a lot of the venues frequented by the former Mi Amigo Drive-In Shows of earlier times. The new shows were always well attended and using the name Radio Caroline went down well with the young audience. Not with the authorities, needless to say, who raided several events, questioning the organisers intently and issuing stern warnings of prosecution.

My sleeping arrangements in Belgium were not particularly comfortable though, as Danny constantly made me sleep on the settee at his mother's house. Blankets and pillows were never provided and as his mother was an early riser, she would vacuum around me at half-past six in the morning, making as much noise as she could in an effort to wake the lazy foreigner. Danny and I had not arrived home until well past three in the morning on most occasions, which made it all the worse. He slumbered away, without interruption, until late afternoon.

I made a very bad investment around this time, and borrowing the deposit from my long-suffering mother, bought a TR7 car, a bright red one; these vehicles were known as the poor man's sports car. Engine wise, it was flawed from the start and I spent a smallfortune trying to get it to run properly.

Even the garage that sold it to me wouldn't look at it. One mechanic at this unprincipled car sales establishment in Sittingbourne told me they had been trying to get rid of it for months as it was a catastrophe. To say they saw me coming is an understatement. One time, I had it repaired at a large BMW dealership in Brussels and even they said it was beyond hope in the long term. I kept the car for a while in the hope of some miracle, but it was to be a costly endeavour.

Danny would sometimes come to England to spread joy amongst the English Caroline team. He stayed at my mother's house in Kent in the spare room. Sadly, his behaviour became a little less gracious than it could have been under the circumstances. Rather than use the loo in the upstairs hallway, he would occasionally head out into the back garden to relieve himself; he was certainly lacking in basic behavioral skills at times.

My sister, Rosemary, was now in the Wrens, based at SHAPE, near Mons in Belgium, and would come home on leave from time to time to see the family. She arrived home one evening after a night out with friends and was climbing the stairs to bed, when she met Danny in his underpants on the way to the garden. I still remember the shrill scream she emitted, so after that episode, I put him in a local bed and breakfast up the road, and out of harm's way. Quite where he spent a penny while staying at the B and B, I have no idea, and would rather not know.

Danny and I were off again looking for new tenders and this time heading for Faversham creek in Kent, on the slim chance that some poor fisherman, down on his luck, would be interested. After all, we could offer two hundred pounds if pushed, but one hundred and fifty was now the norm for a tender carrying only people. No luck that afternoon, but I was complimented on my good English by a local lady after I asked for directions to the harbour entrance; she had noticed the foreign number plate on the car and assumed I was Belgian.

Danny went back to Belgium later that evening and I was dispatched to several ports on the east coast to find new tenders. I drew a blank, having travelled as far as Hull in my undertakings to find a fisherman willing to risk prosecution. How many times I was reported to the police for trying to procure rogue skippers and their dodgy boats, I do not know.

Quite unexpectedly, I was to find a new tender across the road from my mother's house. My friend Terry had run his boat out to the Mi Amigo on many occasions but had run into trouble with the police, so we left his boat alone for the time being. This particular day, he and I had been to Ramsgate and other south-eastern ports, again looking for tenders, and now we had stopped to get some food at my local fish and chip restaurant.

Whilst in the queue, we overheard a conversation in the customer line between two young men discussing whether to take their boat out that night or leave it until the weekend. We pounced and soon had a new tender running from Queenborough on the Isle of Sheppey. Our contact's name was Steve and I drove over to his house the next morning to sort out some details. Normally, if there is a girlfriend or wife involved, they had been known to try and scupper a deal like this. After all, they did not want their other half doing something illegal and risking their livelihood. I could understand that, but this time, Steve's girlfriend was completely happy with the arrangement.

We had many successful runs with Steve but he did have a love affair with sandbanks and we spent many an hour, far out to sea, trying to get off them, engines screaming in protest, as we headed out to the Mi Amigo. Engine breakdowns too were quite normal with Steve, and one night, whilst ploughing through the waters off the north Kent coast on the way to the radioship, the inevitable happened and the engine spluttered to a halt. Steve and Terry spent several hours trying to restart it but to no avail, and we had no choice but to send up the flares. The first two failed to work and it really was third time lucky.

Terry had been cautioned by the police for his Caroline involvement only weeks earlier and was not keen on being caught on this boat with so much proof of our destination. We were loaded down with food, tapes, programming material and dozens of new albums. We argued about what to do and I did not relish going back to the continent to get more money to repeat the operation; but there was no choice this time. Everything went in the sea, except the personal mail for the crew on the Mi Amigo, which I stuffed into pouches in my jacket. Characteristically, bad luck was with us that night, for the tide was now slack and there was no current to take the goods away; we sat right in the middle of the evidence.

Help came from an unexpected quarter in the form of an immense oil tanker. It towered above us as it slid cautiously to within shouting distance; the crew threw a rope over the stern and we set off for Sheerness.

The vessel was about eighty-thousand tonnes, and even at its slowest speed, pulled us along behind as if we were water-skiing. Arriving off the port, we were met by the lifeboat and towed into the harbour where I handed over thirty pounds for RNLI funds. No questions were asked as to our intended destination and I climbed up the metal ladder with some relief and onto the jetty. Reaching the top, my car keys fell out of my pocket and into the water far below.

I set off for home in a taxi to find a spare set and immediately realised that this was the perfect end [sic] to a particularly wretched day.

St. Edmund's School, Canterbury

St. Edmund's School chapel

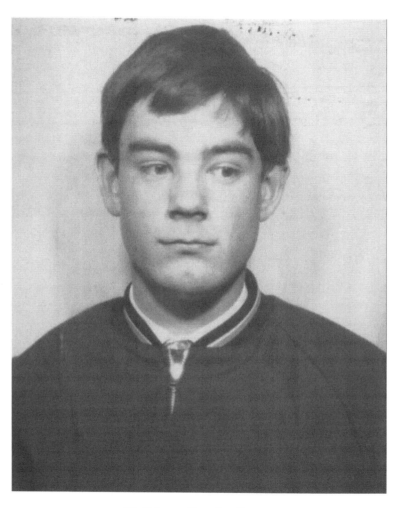

St. Edmund's schoolboy

Home from church on a warm Sunday morning

St. Edmund's schoolboy in London at 13 years old

Nigel in Spain   Ready for school

Nigel on a Spanish beach

(Top and bottom) The summer of 1976 on the North Sea

Nigel in Holland at Radio Day

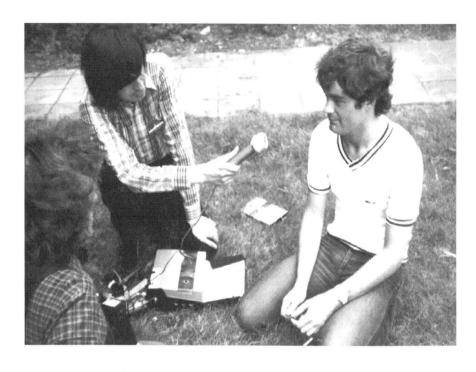

Interview with Stuart Russell at Radio Day in Holland

The Mi Amigo with Frank van der Mast (left)
and Nigel (Stuart Russell)

The Mi Amigo port side deck

Nigel on the Mi Amigo

Mi Amigo, 1976

Stuart Russell (Nigel) in the Mi Amigo messroom*

Tom Anderson, Marc Jacobs and Stuart Russell (Nigel)*

Tony Allan and Stuart Russell in Holland at Radio Day

Marc Jacobs presents the inivitive *'Baken 16'* on Radio Mi Amigo*

Stuart Russell and Belgian sailor, Otto, in the Radio Mi Amigo studio*

Linda the chef, Tom Anderson and Stuart Russell*

The Caroline Roadshow with Robbie Day, Harvey the Rabbit and Robb Eden

The Roadshow on a Summer Tour

British government officials arrive at the Mi Amigo (1979)

The Mi Amigo off Essex in the Knock Deep

Stuart Russell (Nigel) and Samantha in the
Caroline studio

Nigel in the Caroline studio onboard the Mi Amigo

Otto, Kees Borell and Johan Visser in the Mi Amigo messroom

Otto maintains the Mi Amigo's superb paintwork

Sophisticated Caroline presenter, Roger Mathews (r) with Brian Martin*

A relaxed Tony Allan poses for the camera*

The Mi Amigo, late seventies, off the English coast*

Otto, Turkey (cook) and Stuart Russell in disguise as British
government vessel circles the Mi Amigo*

Ad Roberts in Radio Mi Amigo studio*

Herman de Graff

Nigel and Otto in rubberboat

Otto rests after 'hard work' below decks

Otto and Hugo Meulenhoff

Otto and Nigel after a flour fight

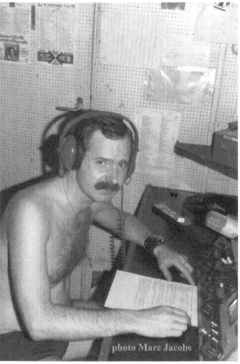

Frank van der Mast *   Herman de Graff*

'I have baked you a cake, you m***** f*****!' says Kees*

Marc Jacobs broadcasts in a fetching pirate outfit*

Kenny Page on Radio Caroline in 1976. He left soon afterwards
for the Voice of Peace in Israel*

Visitors to the Mi Amigo, 1979

Radio Mi Amigo studio onboard the Mi Amigo*

Marc Jacobs presents 'Baken 16'*

Rob Hudson, Luc Watermans (engineer), Kees Borrel and Marc Jacobs*

Stuart Russell and Tom van der Velden; Christmas Dinner on the Mi Amigo

A North Sea summer sunset*

The Mi Amigo's final resting place, March 1980

Trinity House marker buoy close to the wreck of the Mi Amigo

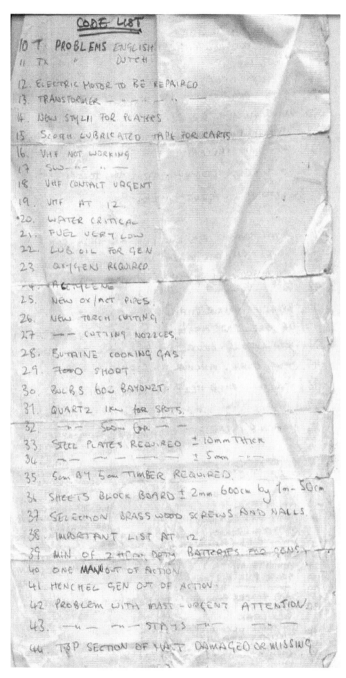

CODE LIST

10 T PROBLEMS ENGLISH
11 Tx " DUTCH

12. ELECTRIC MOTOR TO BE REPAIRED
13. TRANSFORMER — - - - - - -
14. NEW STYLII FOR PLAYERS
15 SCOTCH LUBRICATED TAPE FOR CARTS
16. VHF NOT WORKING
17 SW - - - -
18 UHF CONTACT URGENT
19. UHF AT 12
*20. WATER CRITICAL
21. FUEL VERY LOW
22 LUB OIL FOR GEN
23 OXYGEN REQUIRED
-24 ACETYLENE
25. NEW OX/ACT PIPES
26. NEW TORCH CUTTING
27 — - CUTTING NOZZLES
28. BUTANE COOKING GAS
29. FOOD SHORT
30. BULBS 60S BAYONET
31. QUARTZ 1KW for SPOTS
32 - - 500 GA - -
33 STEEL PLATES REQUIRED ± 10mm THICK
34 - - - - - - - ± 5mm - - -
35 5cm BY 5cm TIMBER REQUIRED
36 SHEETS BLOCK BOARD ± 2mm 600cm by 1m - 50cm
37 SELECTION BRASS WOOD SCREWS AND NAILS
38 IMPORTANT LIST AT 12
39 MIN OF 2 HEAVY DUTY BATTERIES FOR GENS - - -
40 ONE MAN OUT OF ACTION
41 HENSCHEL GEN OUT OF ACTION
42 PROBLEM WITH MAST - URGENT ATTENTION
43 - - - - - STAYS - - - - -
44 TOP SECTION OF MAST DAMAGED OR MISSING

The code list that gave the news of the Mi Amigo's final troubles (1980)

127

Nigel in the messroom onboard Radio Paradise in Dublin

Radio Paradise on the River Liffey in Dublin (1981)

A dirty, smelly job painting huge fuel tanks on the ship

Radio Paradise off the Dutch coast (1981)

Radio Paradise, under arrest, on the way into port after the raid
(1981)

The Ross Revenge on the North Sea (1983)

Captain Ernie Stevenson works on the hull of the Ross Revenge

Tom Anderson (centre) and Nigel (right)

A sunny day onboard the Ross Revenge

Radio Monique's Walter Simons (left) and Colin Peters (right)

Ross Revenge galley

Caroline 558 studio on the Ross Revenge

Captain Ernie and DJ Chris Kennedy on the Ross Revenge

Tim Allen and Pat Brooks onboard the Ross Revenge (1987)

Chris Kennedy, Nigel Harris and Neil Gates

Ross Revenge newsroom and programming office

Messroom at Christmas with storm breaks in place

Dutch DJ Colin Peters on the air at Radio Monique

The Olau ferry passes the Ross Revenge (1989)

50,000 watt transmitter onboard the Ross Revenge

Nigel hopes for a quick trip to the Ross Revenge (1990)

Ross Revenge with twin masts (1990)

The Voice of Peace anchored off the Tel Aviv coast (1991)

The tender alongside the Peaceship off Tel Aviv

Generator spares arrive at the Peaceship

Alex Rogers, centre, and crewmembers onboard the Peaceship

The bus climbing into Jerusalem city

Refueling the Peaceship in Ashdod

Kenny Page onboard the Peaceship as a tender arrives alongside (1991)

CHAPTER 14

We were now heading into autumn and repair work on the ship still did not take place and she continued to suffer. Water would suddenly appear in the corridors downstairs as a section of the hull would spring yet another leak. The call would go out for wood and concrete and we would go in search of the damaged plate, often crawling on our hands and knees through oil and muck in the bilges looking for the latest damage. When it was located, we would continue with our foolproof solution, and hammer a tapered piece of wood into the hole, dry it off and set it in concrete. Great care was taken as to who knew about this operation since some of the crew were understandably anxious and the last thing we needed was to cause alarm.

These leaks were a constant reminder as to the state of the hull but it was not hull damage that caused us to nearly sink one late summer's day; the water came from another source.

I was in the downstairs studio presenting the last hour of my breakfast show. Noticing water in the record library, the call went out saying we had a new leak and yet another search started. But this time, no leak could be located and the ship continued to take on water, so much so that the stern was starting to settle. The pumps were going flat out but they made little difference to the critical condition of the ship.

By about lunchtime, the situation was getting pretty desperate and any liferafts onboard that worked were launched. They were all years past their expiry date and several would not inflate but we could all squeeze into the one larger raft that was in working condition, if it became necessary. The bows of the Mi Amigo were now quite high out of the water and we stood up front looking back down the ship as the stern continued to sink ever lower. It was a sunny day and if we were to lose the ship, the weather could not have been any kinder towards us.

Of course, our predicament had been mentioned on the air earlier in the day, causing panic amongst listeners and in the offices in England and on the continent. By now, we had gone off the air and were in contact with the coastguard, but saying the situation was tolerable for the time being, so there was no need for a lifeboat to come out to us; we would not give up yet.

Eventually, the search for the leak had to be abandoned and there seemed very little we could do except surrender our beautiful old ship to the deep.

Suddenly, much excitement erupted from the doorway to the engine room. Someone shouted, 'We've got it, we've found it!' Everyone left their position and headed for the lower deck. A final desperate attempt to locate the trouble had been executed by one of the crew who had held his head under the water alongside one of the generators long enough to notice some air bubbles; there appeared to be a leak in one of the cooling pipes for the generators. This was closed off and the pumps eventually managed to get hold of the situation, with the Mi Amigo coming back onto an even keel within hours.

Outside on deck, we noticed a plane coming towards us and as it swept low, we could see faces frantically peering down onto the ship. We all waved, trying to convey the fact that we would be alright after all. It was a plane sent out by the Belgian office to see what was happening far out on the North Sea. We found out later that they had misconstrued our waving motions for that of panic; it meant they experienced a frightful flight back home before hearing the news that the ship would be safe after all.

We were lucky that time, but the serious leaks from the hull were now getting more and more regular. Winter was approaching and we knew the gales were not far away, which filled us with a feeling of gloom and anguish.

Tenders were again being stopped and searched and boat owners warned of severe penalties if caught supplying the Mi Amigo.

In Belgium, the authorities were starting to clamp down hard on advertisers and they were on a bit of a high as they had successfully seen off the new Radio Mi Amigo ship, the Magdalena, which experienced a troubled short life anchored off the Belgian coast.

Meanwhile, we were running more and more food, water and people out from Brightlingsea with the anorak boat trips than ever before; it kept our continental vessels free of the supplies and people that would certainly give the game away if confronted. So, this way, in the event of any boats being stopped, only fuel would be found on board.

Another supply run was due on the Saturday from England and I set off with my mum's mini packed to the hilt with food and drink. No crew change was scheduled this time, making things easier for me, however, I needed to go into London to see Ronan before going to the coast. Bearing in mind I had not slept for a couple of days, having just returned from Belgium with money for the supplies and the tender, I was feeling a little world-weary and battle-scarred.

After Ronan, the next stop was a little house way off in the Hertfordshire countryside to collect more bits for the ship; friends of Albert and Georgina had kindly donated more goodies to be taken to the boys at sea. Only ten minutes into this section of the journey, a sharp bend in the road with a high muddy kerb took me by surprise and sent the car over onto two wheels and then on its side. Washing powder, breakfast cereals and lemonade combined into a thick gooey mess inside the car and left me buried under dozens of boxes, carrier bags and loose potatoes.

Managing to extradite myself through the passenger door and out of the car, I took stock of the situation and with a mighty heave, attempted to right the vehicle. Even for five strong men, it would have been a challenge but for me it was impossible. After a long walk back to the house I had recently left, taking several hours, more favours were called in; a tractor came out to the accident site and after righting the car, we towed it away and I sheepishly went home by train to face my mother, whilst the boat went to sea with only the anoraks on board and no supplies.

There is an upside to all this; our tender was searched on the way out to Radio Caroline by the Essex police. They found nothing, whilst my mum's battered little mini went to the local garage for repairs.

As the winter months drew in, the Mi Amigo rode out a couple of storms with little damage and we all had a good Christmas; three Christmas trees that year, and a few more leaks to keep us on our toes. I left the ship on shore leave after the New Year celebrations and nineteen-eighty got underway with a couple of new advertisers on the Dutch service, which somewhat boosted moral.

Tendering was still a major problem for us as the Belgian police were now stopping our fuel tenders three times out of four as they headed our way from the continent. No proof was found as to the destination of the boats, but the owners were warned that severe penalties would follow if they were caught supplying the Mi Amigo. This was enough to deter them.

We continued to get food, water and people, now including the Dutch, out from England while all efforts went into finding another large vessel to get some significant amounts of fuel and water delivered to the Mi Amigo. Everyone we approached had been warned off along the Dutch and Belgian coasts and we were treated by some fishing crews as if we were trying to recruit personnel for a vicious terrorist attack.

Perseverance did pay off eventually and we found a willing partner. Our new tender skipper gambled on doing a few runs with his boat, the Hosanna, to help ward off repossession of his house by the bank.

The bonus this time was that the authorities knew nothing about our new supplier, so it was safe bet that we could get away with it for a little while. We managed a few runs from this cash-starved fisherman and bunkered the tanks on our ship; we then rested him as we had enough fuel for many weeks.

Exhausted, I returned to England to have a few days rest. Later that week, I was told to go back to Belgium immediately because something dramatic had happened. That evening, I sat in a bar with Danny, listening with disbelief to his account.

Our tender, the Hosanna, whilst on a break from supplying the Mi Amigo, had been at sea attempting to get a decent haul of fish. The crew had set off a couple of days earlier from Zeebrugge and then disappeared; no more contact whatsoever had been made with land.

That morning, wreckage had been found, with a lifejacket floating nearby, but no sign of life. My heart sank and I felt shocked and unable to speak for a moment. 'What happened?' I murmured. Danny said that nobody really knew, but he had some suspicions. He thought it was an insurance scam as the skipper was in so much financial trouble. I hoped this was right and the crew were all alive somewhere, planning their next move.

Danny decided a good way of finding out was to visit the skipper's wife. This was a bad idea and I did not feel at ease with it, so I tried, without luck, to talk him out of the plan.

The next morning, we were in a small sitting room having tea with a desperately unhappy woman who cried with such grief and anguish, I was getting more and more upset. This insurance scam idea seemed even less likely when she said her fourteen year old son was onboard when the boat disappeared.

I really thought there was no way Danny's idea could be the reason for the boat's disappearance, but if it was a scam, the man's wife was a pretty good actress.

No fraudulent claims were ever made, no bodies ever found, but sadly, the fishing boat was discovered on the seabed off the Goodwin Sands. She had been hit by another vessel, although the offending ship was never located; the missing fishermen were eventually declared dead.

CHAPTER 15

Studios on board the Mi Amigo were now virtually inoperative and were held together with rubber bands and string. Cart machines did not work and the Revox reel-to-reel tape machines were all without workable motors. The repair bills would be vast, so it was decided to do a little at a time and fix things in small batches. But more money was required, as the little we had all went into fuel, water and food plus the cost of the tenders. Conditions on board continued to deteriorate. There was very little fresh water for washing and no heating onboard. All cooking was done in seawater and personal hygiene became secondary with half a sink full of tepid water in which to bathe, but only on the odd occasion.

My friend Terry and I headed for Leysdown, on the Isle of Sheppey, to visit a nightclub owner whom we thought might part with some money for advertising. We left the club feeling quietly confident after a cautious agreement to advertise had been thrashed out. We assured our man that if he had any problems with the authorities, an advertisement in the local Kent Messenger newspaper was the way out. His advert would be published in the paper and would just coincidentally be read out on the air, so he could deny any connection with us.

It was time to go back to Belgium and I picked up more cash for food and tenders and came back to England with a new Dutch presenter called Ton Lathouwers to help with programming. The Dutch service had suffered badly over the last few weeks due to staff shortages and it was getting difficult to find new recruits. Word had spread throughout the industry in Holland and Belgium as to the condition of the ship and people considered their lives would be put at risk by going to sea.

It was now March, nineteen-eighty and soon we would be into spring and a start could be made on getting things ship-shape again. The shore team went shopping and spent a good deal more on food than was usual, causing raised eyebrows in the local Sainsbury's supermarket in Sittingbourne. Alcohol and cigarettes always had to be bought, so careful balancing of the budget was essential. I was going to the ship on a return trip, hoping to come back with some selected equipment requiring repair.

Steve was our boatman again this time and we headed for Queenborough harbour and boarded the boat. The weather forecast was not good for the next couple of days but we thought we could just about get a run in if we were speedy in our endeavours. Turning for the open sea, a wave breaking over the bow hit me full on as I tidied up some ropes, causing me to reel back across the deck and into the wheelhouse. Still within sight of land, I was soaked to the skin; my desperate urge to get wet on these tender runs was as keen as ever.

The journey was slow and bumpy and we heaved our way through the dirty brown confused seas. Our boat took on a fair amount of water, but we managed to ease things a little by steering around some of the bigger waves. By the time we were alongside the Mi Amigo, the weather was closing in and it was getting a lot rougher with heavy seas churning around the two vessels. The ropes strained hard as they held the tender to the radioship and how long they would last under this fierce pressure was a major concern, so we had to quicken our work. I had gathered cart machines and other electrical equipment in the messroom to bring ashore. A petrol generator had to go for repair and we managed to manhandle the alternator section over the heaving waves and onto the tender. Steve, on the smaller boat, was getting more concerned about the weather so we had to pick up the pace even more. Food was transferred and boxes of records and paperwork made it over too. It was now too rough to do very much else but we tried to get an empty gas bottle ashore; this proved to be so difficult, the attempt was abandoned. 'Leave the rest of it,' I shouted across the crashing waves and gestured to those coming ashore to get onto the tender immediately. Dutch presenter Ad Roberts clambered over but I decided to stay on the Mi Amigo. I asked Steve to come back when the weather improved; but at the last moment, I decided against it as I really needed go to Belgium for more money, so we left Tom Anderson, Nick Richards, Stevie Gordon and newcomer Ton onboard whilst we headed back to land through the worsening waves. I watched the Mi Amigo as she fought the heavy seas and we turned to face land, knowing this was to be yet another insufferable journey.

Due to the bad weather and the rolling and pitching of the small fishing boat, our propeller seemed to be out of the water more than churning through the seas. It was constantly screaming as it sought the water it required to propel us homeward. I had been in rough seas before and thought I had seen it all but this time I was fearful and somewhat scared. I began to think we'd never make land.

I shouted to Terry in a high pitched voice, 'We're not going survive this, are we?' I just needed someone to say it would be alright, even if it were a lie. Terry's face was as panic-stricken as mine and he shouted back over the deafening commotion in the wheelhouse that if we could survive the next few hours, we might just get away with it. Not the comforting words I had hoped to hear.

We ploughed on southwards through the mighty green rollers of the North Sea; we had been on our homeward journey for several hours now. The seas smashed into the little wheelhouse with thundering force and we huddled together in the ominous dusk whilst I silently prayed that we'd make landfall soon.

Then the inevitable happened, as if things could get any worse; the engine gave up the ghost and ground to a halt, having been flooded one time too many. We were at the mercy of the elements with no way of correcting our position, and inevitably, we now turned sideways onto these huge waves. Sheer fear flowed throughout my body as our skipper Steve pulled open the hatchway to the engine compartment and climbed inside. It was like being in a barrel going over Niagara Falls, I imagined, as we climbed sideways up each wave and fell down the other side. I had no time to be seasick; absolute terror had taken over as we all clung on for dear life. I began to find it difficult to breath as panic flooded through my body. I wished with all my heart I'd stayed on the Mi Amigo.

After about half-an-hour, I was to make a stupid decision that was to very nearly cost me my life. I desperately needed to answer a call of nature, so I fought open the doorway onto the back deck and stood in the howling wind and spray looking for a safe place to go. The door onto the deck caught the wind and slammed wide open before being grabbed by those inside and pulled shut.

I should have peed on the deck, let the sea wash it away, then climbed back inside rapidly, but I didn't. The others huddled in the wheelhouse as Steve fought to restart the engine. Outside, I stood on the side of the boat in the howling wind, holding on with one hand to a rail on the wheelhouse and answering the call into the North Sea.

Instead of stepping back into the boat and zipping up, I let go of the rail to do so, before fully getting to safety. As soon as my hand left the rail, I was pitched into the heaving seas and disappeared beneath the waves. I remember the sensation of going under the water and nothing more until I bobbed up again a little way behind the stern of the boat as another huge wave lifted us all up. Although I was in trouble, I felt no fear and just resigned to the fact I was going to drown.

My guardian angel was certainly with me that day because as I went over the side, those in the wheelhouse noticed that I had disappeared from view and immediately struggled out onto the deck, just as I rose up behind the boat. Being held by his legs, Terry managed to reach out into the sea with a boathook and snare the hood of my jacket, gradually dragging me back towards the stern. Many hands reached out and I was pulled to safety. With no working engine and the radio out of action, had this one attempt to grab me failed, I would have drifted away in the storm and that would have been my end.

I was hauled back into the wheelhouse, undressed and wrapped in dry but dirty towels to try to warm up. I shook with cold and shock but the fear of the boat sinking had eased somewhat as it was now my saviour and deliverance from a freezing death in the North Sea.

There was still another hour or so to go before Steve managed to get the engine fired up again, albeit very half-heartedly and with much smoke and backfiring.

He had nursed it back to life by some means and we got underway again and turned for land. The mountainous seas continued to pummel the little fishing boat and began demolishing parts of the wheelhouse and decking whilst ripping fishing winches from their mountings and discarding them in the sea as if they were matchwood.

The boat had become bow heavy in the howling north-easterly winds and had taken on a pretty large amount of water. Several members of the party were dispatched to sit out on the back end of the aft deck; this extra weight enabling the propellers to bite into the sea a little better. They clung on for dear life as the stricken vessel haphazardly crawled ever forward towards land.

It was determined that instead of going around the northern side of the Isle of Sheppey and into the Thames Estuary, we would head around the back of the island and into calmer waters. This was to add another few hours to our already demanding journey but eventually it took us into Queenborough, almost fifteen hours after we had first set off for the North Sea.

The boat tied up on its mooring in the middle of the river and the crew were ferried one at a time to shore with Terry taking charge of a small rowing-boat. When at last it was my turn to leave, I clambered into the tiny craft with Terry and we set off for the jetty. We managed to get halfway to the shore before we were suddenly caught in an unexpected but strong mid-channel current and as Terry struggled determinedly against the force of the water, we were carried off down river and away from our destination. I was no help at all as not an ounce of strength remained in my body after the appalling exploits out at sea.

At long last, after much struggling and fortitude, Terry managed to get the boat out of the current and we made it to shore, a long way downriver. As far as I was concerned, we were home at last. Still in shock, I sat in the stinking mud on the riverside, soaking wet and shivering violently. I held my head in my hands and fell to one side, crying with a combination of relief and despair. After a while, I joined the others as we started out on our various journeys home. We did not know it yet, but what lay in store would put recent events in the shade.

CHAPTER 16

The events of the day before had left me somewhat traumatised and it was not something I would tell my mother about as she would have worried too much about future trips. However, there was no time to relax because by late afternoon, our system of code numbers from the ship was causing us great concern. I heard the numbers in the late afternoon announced between the recorded Dutch programmes and went to my code sheet with some trepidation. We had recently devised a new list, so these numbers were a little unfamiliar to me, although my worst fears were confirmed; the anchor chain had broken. Further confirmation came in a phone call from Robb Eden in London; he was in contact with Ronan.

There was no hope of getting a boat out to the Mi Amigo in the stormy conditions and no way of getting in touch with the ship. The only news came with updated code numbers being read out on a regular basis. The ship carried a spare anchor strapped to the starboard side which could be cut loose when required and I hoped this would be possible before the ship hit any sandbanks or came within British waters. The storm was increasing in intensity as Terry and I set off for Margate coastguard station in the hope of being able to talk to our friends on the ship. We set off in my dreaded TR7 and on this of all nights, the car continued to plague me; after all the dire events that had happened lately, I certainly did not want us to get stranded on the side of the motorway.

The car stalled and backfired all the way to the coast but we got there eventually and made our way up to see the coastguard. He was getting up-to-date information on the emergency channel from Tom Anderson out at sea on the Mi Amigo. But this coastguard was also a stickler for the letter of the law, and he told us it was illegal for us to speak to Tom; we would have to leave and this we reluctantly did. The Sheerness lifeboat was now on its way to the Mi Amigo and the boys onboard were describing their plight in more detail on the air.

The spare anchor had gone over the side but had held the ship right on the edge of a sandbank, rather than in deeper waters. By now, the story was making television and radio news across Europe and we sat in my TR7 in Margate looking out to sea, incalculably worried about our friends. Now of all times, this disaster-prone car refused to start and we had to leave it in Margate and get a taxi home, where my mum's car was again called into service. We headed at speed for Sheerness.

With no precise idea of where to meet the crew when they came ashore and knowing access to the Dockyard would be subject to scrutiny, we waited at the police station in town. I began thinking about the ship and what could be happening to her out at sea. I prayed the pumps would cope with any water coming in and wondered if and when we could get out to her again.

The guys from the ship had come ashore with the lifeboat, the Helen Turnbull, and been taken to Sheerness police station for questioning. The rescue was the most difficult ever achieved by the Sheerness lifeboat and it took many attempts to get alongside the ship and evacuate the crew. The seas were horrendous and the lifeboat crew were heroes in achieving a successful outcome. The skipper, Charlie Bowry, was later given an award for the heroic rescue.

Our guys were released within hours from custody, apart from Tom Anderson who had missed a court appearance whilst at sea for a minor offence and was now facing the consequences with continued police questioning.

Robb Eden had arrived and we all headed for the service station on the M2 near Gillingham for some food and warm drinks. The rescued crew had more terrifying tales to tell of huge seas and brave lifeboat men struggling to get their rescue craft alongside the Mi Amigo. But it was good to know that our little canary had managed to come ashore rather than face what the dark night might bring. The rescued men, now including Tom, could not wait to get home and were soon ferried to railway stations for their respective journeys.

We all promised to get in touch later in the day and I went home and eventually fell into a deep sleep.

It was my mum who woke me about fours hours later and suggested I get up and watch the news on television. I grabbed a cup of tea just in time for the one o'clock news and stood nervously in front of the television.

Even before a word had been uttered, the pictures answered all my questions. The pumps had not coped and the Mi Amigo had foundered on the edge of the sandbank where she was held in place by her emergency anchor. The top of the bridge, forepeak, bowsprit and some of the upper superstructure were still visible above the swirling seas. But the saddest thing about the pictures was the mast, still standing proudly above the sunken ship, almost oblivious to the chaos that had taken place below. The Mi Amigo, after all her miraculous escapes of the past, was lost.

I felt heartbroken, as did so many others. Tears welled up in my eyes and I wept for my poor radioship, my life for so many years. I felt desperate, but so relieved that nobody had died. The magnificent Mi Amigo would never have allowed that to happen. She had waited until everybody was safely off on the lifeboat before finally giving up on the Long Sand.

A reporter from the local daily paper, the Evening Post, came round to my house later that afternoon for an interview, which appeared the next day. The national press carried the story in detail, with the Daily Telegraph mourning Caroline's departure in a leader column. It read:

'One of the neglected 'lieder' of Mozart contains the line, "When I Kiss My Little Caroline." The words are about par for the course where pop music is concerned. The song has never won the approval of discerning classical musicologists because of its dull and predictable harmonies. There are those who would charge pop with dull and predictable melodies. However, we must all mourn the other Caroline now lying in the silt off Clacton, having, as it were, laughed all the way to the Dogger Bank. She has cheekily provided a service at a profit giving people what they wanted and raising advertising revenue in the process.' [sic]

The article concludes, *'How different this pirate has been to the respectable Admiralty version, Radio One, which in a sellers' market gives away what could be sold and then demands a licence subsidy to cover its philanthropy. Radio One will not sink. It makes no money, provides no service distinguishable from those of commercial popular stations. As for the radio that does give an independent original service, our Mozartian Radio Karolinchen (Radio Three), it does not sink either, but slips into tubercular decline, rotting half a grain a day as the number of original transmissions is cut back. Caroline has gone down in the North Sea; Radio Three is at the mercy of an element not so rough but almost as wet.'* (Daily Telegraph, Saturday, March 22nd, 1980)

Elsewhere, there was no time to waste, and plans got underway for a replacement ship. Energy was high in those early weeks after the sinking and back in the eighties, starting an offshore radio station was still within the realms of possibility.

However, the time dragged on and days rolled into weeks and I needed to earn some money. Rumours of new ships abounded and stories that the Mi Amigo would be raised from the seabed popped up from time to time.

Nothing positive seemed to be happening and little by little, the team broke up. But it was not in my nature to give up on Radio Caroline and I toured many a shipyard looking for a potential radioship. Independently, it was an unrewarding task, but very soon, a little help was at hand.

CHAPTER 17

A former Mi Amigo land-based crewmember Peter Moore and I joined forces and went looking for potential radioships in various ports in southeast England. We had hoped to kick-start the organisation by finding a vessel that could be used for Radio Caroline. We toured ship after ship, but none seemed entirely right. One we did like had no working engine, therefore she was in a scrap yard in Sittingbourne, and with the cost of repair too high, we declined the offer to buy.

Another project underway around the same time was the Phoenix Radio Project, involving the *Birchlea*, a former fishing trawler, bought for £5000 through a broker in Ramsgate and berthed in Aberdeen. A relative of Roger Mathews had raised the money for this boat and we transported a new generator by road to Aberdeen. This was not a Caroline undertaking but we had a good team involved with Roger, Bob Lawrence and Peter Moore. Terry Purvis was our skipper and we all set off to view our floating acquisition.

The team, now including another former Mi Amigo land-based crewmember, Terry, arrived in Aberdeen in the middle of a snowstorm, again in my mother's little red mini, after a long and difficult journey lasting the best part of twenty hours. Peter Moore made his own way up and joined us after a short while. Locating the boat was not too difficult, although there were dozens of identical vessels berthed all the way down the quayside. When I spotted our boat moored on the jetty, the snow falling heavily on the deck, my heart sank; she did not look big enough to handle the dangerous storms that the North Sea could dish out. But youthful exuberance took over, and we climbed aboard, torches blazing in the dark interior. Being exceptionally tired, we threw sleeping bags into the bridge and tried to sleep in the bitter cold. It was an impossible task and we chatted on and off all night about this new project; the more we conversed, the more the problems grew.

Roger Mathews had been into Aberdeen one cold evening and came back with an engineer who had agreed to work on the ship whilst we were in port. They arrived back on the ship long after midnight and I had already gone to bed in one of the ship's cabins on the upper deck, fully clothed and wrapped up in numerous sleeping bags. The coldness of the Scottish air bit into every fibre of my being and getting to sleep took an age.

Sleep was very soon interrupted when I received a rude awakening; a bright torch shone in my face. I was told by the new engineer that he wanted the cabin, as he was my superior. I sat up in bed to see that he had a young boy with him. I assumed it was his son, but not on this occasion. Our new engineer told me he was a married man who had woken up a few weeks earlier and decided he was gay. He said he had now left his wife and was having a wild time catching up on things he should have done years before, although I'm not sure I believed his story. As I got out of bed, complaining bitterly, but not wanting an argument, the engineer announced that I could stay. Thinking he had changed his mind, I climbed back into my bunk, whilst the newcomer proceeded to sit alongside me and snuggle up. It was to be a threesome; I declined the offer and left them to it.

I had to spend the night in a freezing cabin below deck with my sleeping bags and a small Calor gas heater for warmth. It was akin to a prisoner-of-war camp downstairs, with brown metal bunks slung alongside the cold metal walls of the large communal cabin.

Nobody slept well that night and at first light we set about getting our new generator installed in the engine room. This equipment had been brought up on the back of a trailer from Kent, having been bought from an advertisement I had seen in Exchange and Mart magazine.

Aberdeen was experiencing one of the coldest winters on record and pipes froze onboard even during the daylight hours. We finally managed to get the lights on and some limited heating in diminutive areas around the ship; we soon felt a little better.

Within a day or two, after extensive work on our systems, a discovery was made that could have scuppered the whole project even before it got underway; the main engine did not work, as the bearings were shattered. We had been misled over this rather important matter when we bought the vessel.

Again, only a lot of expensive work could solve the problem and that was out of the question. The project had been put together without anyone really going into the feasibilities of the whole objective. We were a bunch of enthusiastic amateurs with very little experience in fitting out a radioship, and even less money. Another laughable purchase was the transmitter, bought for one thousand pounds from an unidentified man in Kent and delivered in kit form in six large boxes; it was optimistically hoped this hotchpotch gathering of bits and pieces would deliver five kilowatts.

We got to know various people up and down the jetty in Aberdeen who thought we had bought the vessel for research purposes and when told we had no working engines, a deal was done for us to take over the *Cedarlea*, sister ship of the Birchlea, moored a little further down the dock and in far better condition. The Cedarlea was formerly known as the Ross Beaver, and was part of the same fleet as the Ross Revenge, soon to be the new Radio Caroline ship. But this change of vessel cost us even more precious money, and there was hardly any left for our radio project.

The plan was to bring the boat to Queenborough in Kent, and complete a refit before setting out to sea. In our own back yard, we could take our time and cut costs by completing much of the work ourselves.

A few weeks later, I came back to Kent to ready the manpower and set the location for the ship, whilst the Cedarlea crew set off into the North Sea for the journey south. After a day or two at sea, a huge bank of fog descended across the water and our intrepid band of warriors deemed it best to make land and headed into Harwich.

Once there, the ship was impounded and our organisation disbanded. The authorities had got wind of our venture and when word reached them that the ship was in Harwich, they pounced. However, the ship itself did have a better future; Greenpeace, the environmental organisation, bought the vessel in ninety eighty-two, and put her to good use for several years. Under the command of Ken Ballard, she, along with the Sirius, '*tracked down a fleet of Dutch ships, attempting the largest sea dump ever undertaken in the heart of the rich fishing grounds off the Northwest coast of Spain. In a five week period during August and September, 1982, four cargo ships were to dump some 15,000 tonnes of nuclear waste from the UK, Belgium, the Netherlands and Switzerland. Greenpeace was determined to do all it could to hinder this operation.*' (source: Greenpeace)

As the Cedarlea could not be an offshore radio station, it was good to know that our intrepid little vessel was now involved in something this honourable.

Days later, news came through that there were serious events happening with the new Caroline ship, the Ross Revenge, in Spain. But before I could get involved in that drama, if allowed of course, an offer came from Holland to join yet another organisation attempting to get a radioship to sea.

CHAPTER 18

I lay in bed one morning several days later thinking about the Voice of Peace, anchored off Israel. So many friends had gone there after the Mi Amigo sank and the time now seemed right. I decided to get in touch with James Ross, who had gone to the Peaceship long before the Mi Amigo sinking episode. I needed to find out the procedure involved in getting to Tel Aviv and out to the ship. But as usual, I did not get motivated very quickly and several days went by before I had the urge to do something constructive.

It was just after lunch when the phone rang. I had been in the park playing with my dog, Mandy, who was enjoying the fact I was at home for a good deal of the time.

I knew the call was from abroad by the funny pulsing sound that always preceded the actual connection; I had heard it so many times before in my dealings with Holland and Belgium.

It was Ben Bode, who had been involved with Danny Vuylsteke and Freddie Bolland in the last few months of the Dutch service of Radio Caroline.

'How are you? Are you working now?' he asked. I explained the present situation and he sounded pleased to hear that I was doing very little. 'I have work for you, if you'd like it,' he exclaimed. Even before I knew what it was, I muttered a form of acceptance. There was a ship in Cuxhaven, northern Germany, being readied for the North Sea as an offshore radio station. I was to be paid one hundred pounds a week and would work on the ship during its conversion into a broadcasting vessel. My decision to join the organisation was to cause me many months of toil and anguish, but at least there was some money available this time.

I was off into the unknown yet again and accordingly packed my bags and set off on the ferry for Calais. Then it was a train journey to Amsterdam and a car ride into Germany to join the ship; this was the Radio Paradise saga. It was the beginning of a new escapade and those concerned were initially in high spirits. Our first port of call was the bank where Ben drew out a huge amount of money to pay for the tow through the locks and out to the open sea. I sat in the corner at a small desk watching the goings on in this German bank.

It was my first time in Germany and there was plenty to see. Cuxhaven is a large town on the shore of the North Sea at the mouth of the Elbe

River and I wandered around the town for an hour or two before dinner.

We ate at a fine restaurant that night and I got my first glimpse of this new radioship in the lights along the harbour wall. She was the Magda Maria, bigger than the Mi Amigo and still a cargo-ship; no work had yet been done on her conversion. An anchor chain ran from the chain locker up on to the bow and out onto the quayside. Alongside this, lay what I presumed to be the ship's large heavy anchor to be used when we eventually started broadcasting from the North Sea.

The next morning, we were scheduled to leave Germany under total secrecy, make our way towards the North Sea, and then follow the English Channel, heading west. We were going to Dublin for the refit.

There were several locks to negotiate on the way to the sea, and although this was a secret mission, I did spot a photographer taking pictures as we slowly moved along the waterways.

I had my own cabin onboard and set about making it as comfortable as possible, as this venture looked as if it could be a long haul. It wasn't a large room, but big enough for my limited amount of luggage. My old friend Kees Borrell, the cook from the Mi Amigo, had joined us in the new venture. The galley would be his domain, along with helping us with the conversion.

Ben Bode was a tall man, at least six and a half feet, with thick bottle-like glasses and an abrupt manner. This may have manifested itself more in his second language, English, than when he spoke in his native Dutch. I soon discovered that if I was given something to do by this man, I had better do it and do it quickly, or suffer his wrath. He had a temper the like of which I had not seen in a long time and could fly off the handle at the slightest hiccup in the proceedings. But on reflection, he had a lot of responsibility on his shoulders and there was a lot at risk.

We cleared the lock system after several hours and eventually headed out to sea. It was exciting to be involved in this new radio project and as we headed down the coast, I thought that life was starting to improve.

We continued steaming along the English coast on our way to Dublin, a fine city by all accounts, but not one to which I'd given too much thought yet; it had a cathedral and that would be worth a look when we got there. I did not know how much free time I would have after the real work started, but weekends promised to be a little less busy. There was a deadline of three months to get the work done and leave harbour before the authorities became too aware of the situation.

Meals were held in the modest messroom with its mahogany

woodwork throughout; there was a hatchway leading directly into the galley which made things easier for feeding the crew. Onboard with Ben, Kees and me were an assortment of German crewmembers who would go home once we docked at Dublin.

We sailed along the Dutch and Belgian coasts and through the Straits of Dover, hardly believing our luck as the weather held and the predicted winds did not really materialise. But later in the evening as we continued our passage westward towards Dublin, the seas became incredibly rough off the south coast of England. As we passed Brighton, the ship was ploughing into exceptionally large waves sending frightening shudders from one end of the vessel to the other. I did not know this ship or how it would handle in bad weather, so I was concerned.

The Magda Maria was being flung in every direction as I clung onto furniture in the messroom. Then Ben ordered me to the engine room to go on watch. 'Why?' I queried as we were thrown across the room. Ben shouted his reply above the increasing din of the storm. 'The engine keeps cutting out so go to the engine room and watch for problems!'

This turned out to be a dreadful combination of noise, the smell of diesel, seasickness and the inability to remain in any one position for long as the ship crashed about in the stormy seas. I watched this pig of an engine as it noisily clanked in and out of life every few minutes. Eventually, it gave up totally, and we sat in the English Channel at the full mercy of this brutal storm.

I thought at the time that these idiots running the ship must have known the weather would be bad at some point along the way, but had decided to make a run for it.

A rescue tug was called and the Magda Maria was taken into Southampton for repairs. Getting out of the storm and into harbour that night was a blessing; something for which I had been praying.

Naturally, this whole rescue exercise cost a fortune but within three days we were on our way again. The journey up through the Irish Sea was bumpy but tolerable and our target was soon in sight. We turned into Dublin Bay, passing Dalkey and Dun Laoghaire on our left and soon I could see the twin towers of the power plant with their striking red and white striped top sections. A sight that would greet me every morning as I looked down the River Liffey from the ship; always there like friendly twin sisters.

We docked against the North Wall of the river and tied up, looking to all intents and purposes like any one of the other vessels that came and went. We had moored adjacent to one of the river's many pubs and although it was early in the morning, the bar was open to satisfy the thirst of the many dockyard workers at the end of their nightshift.

An establishment like this would have seen quite an assortment of oddbods over the years with many nationalities coming ashore, so we hoped we would not stand out too much. But we did. An astonishing hush descended on the place as we walked through the double doors and across to the bar. Two Dutchmen, three Germans and an Englishman were now amongst the Irish regulars and it was to be twenty-four pints later between us before we finally retired to the ship.

The troubles in Ireland were at a serious level when we arrived in the port. Bobby Sands, an IRA man, was on hunger strike in prison, determined to starve himself to death for the Republican cause. Ben thought any English people would be shot on sight in Dublin, or kidnapped at the very least, so I was banned from going into town for several weeks before he realised his decision was a little draconian.

When I was allowed into Dublin, Ben told me to put on an American accent if I had to talk. Dress was important too, and I was not allowed to wear the trousers I sometimes wore on the boat for work, for they looked a little like army combat pants so I might be mistaken for a member of the British forces and shot dead where I stood. I did not argue with Ben's illogical theories.

Staying in touch and calling mum on the phone was difficult from Ireland, as all foreign calls had to go through the operator and that meant a journey to the General Post Office in Dublin City and a long wait in a queue for a vacant booth. The phone lines were very crackly and conversations were difficult.

One afternoon after a particularly strenuous morning's work on the ship, I wandered into town, a distance of about two miles, to call home. On entering the GPO building, there was a massive explosion outside the main entrance, followed by screeching sirens and panic-stricken shoppers shouting and screaming as they ran to and from the post office. In the main road, O'Connell Street, a double-decker bus burned out of control and people ran for cover in all directions. I did not have a clue what to do and decided the safest thing was to remain inside the building, away from the bus and the fire, until the situation eased. The majority of people in the bank stayed where they were as the clear-up operation continued outside; eventually the all-clear came, along with the very welcome news that nobody in the vicinity of the incident had been seriously hurt.

CHAPTER 19

Work was hard, as we had a whole ship to convert. The complete hull had to be primed and painted, fuel and water tanks had to be installed and three studios were to be built in the hold. Apart from these major conversions, a hundred and one smaller things had to be done, including the installation of glass windows between the studios and welding latches onto the bulwarks for the mast stays. We worked twelve hours a day in muck and filth, always covered from head to foot in paint and fuel, or any number of odd liquids, foam or gunge that this ship continued to puke out.

We were all tired and frequent arguments broke out onboard over the most trivial of matters and that drained the team even more. I became nervous around Ben as his mood swings became more unpredictable and on many occasions, decided to call it a day and go home. I always thought better of it in the morning and after all, having been through so much, it would have been a shame to give up before the work was completed.

Ben came back to the ship one afternoon with a fellow who was a few years younger than me, saying that he was joining the crew as a deckhand and would sail with the ship when the work was completed. His name was Kris and he had lost an eye in a fight several years earlier, which did not seem to bother him, as he considered himself quite the streetwise man of Dublin. He was to share a cabin with me and took the vacant top bunk. Kris turned out to be good friend and we got on well, in fact like two schoolboys trying to better the master, in this case, Ben. But very soon, Kris also became a little wary of the powerful booming voice of Ben and his tantrums.

I was allowed to go back to England once every month for two days with the flight paid for by the company and I looked forward to these breaks with great anticipation. Travelling took up a good deal of the time but it was so good to get back to my own bed and see my friends for a day or two. The short breaks were over all too quickly though, but I consoled myself with the thought that all the hard work would be finished at some point and we would have a new radio station at sea.

Back in Dublin, things were becoming really gruesome with so many dirty jobs that needed doing, resulting in very little time to relax. The work was hard; it was mundane and virtually the same, day in, day out.

One Friday night, as we wandered back to the ship after an hour or two in the pub, things were to liven up a little bit with the arrival of the local ladies of the night. A couple of prostitutes were perched at the end of the gangplank, watching as we sauntered towards the ship. 'Hello boys,' said one, almost as a whisper. 'Got a drink for us? We'd love to come onboard.' The greetings were really just a group of worn out clichés and I laughed out loud. Immediately, I was admonished for my rudeness by Ben.

He was very protective of his ship and even though these ladies were definitely not government representatives, he was reluctant to let anyone get to know us or the ship. The girls must have been pretty desperate for cash because they did not give up and followed us up the gangplank and onto the deck.

A little more pleading and they managed to get an invitation inside. None of this held any fascination for me and after making some tea, I left them to it, went to my cabin and climbed into my bunk.

Very soon, as I was on the point of dropping off to sleep, the door opened and I heard whispering. 'He's asleep; he sleeps like a baby, so don't worry.' Kris was in the cabin with one of the goodtime girls.

I had to lie underneath this sex starved boy and a hooker whilst they satisfied each other. It was quite obvious to me that Kris was not as experienced as he had led us to believe, as this girl, whose ample backside I was separated from by only a flimsy piece of chipboard, kept begging, 'Are you done yet?' Puffing and panting, Kris kept repeating, 'Nearly there!'

This went on for about twenty minutes and I think she too was getting bored. I couldn't wait for him to finish either but it went on and on. Then, at last, the gasp that signalled the finalé arrived and I felt as exhilarated as he did, albeit for a different reason. But alas, that was not to be the end; Kris wanted to do it again and offered to pay the same amount for a second session. My mind sank, for I was tired and wanted to go to sleep. I kept thinking, as the pounding continued, that I should get paid by Kris too.

But the little blighter even wanted a third go when this one was over. I was on the point of leaping out of bed to end this debacle, when she said she would only give him a hand-job. I lay back again and closed my eyes. Surely this time, it would be over pretty quickly.

I gave Kris a real telling off in the morning but he thought it was hilarious and insisted I must have enjoyed it too. When Ben found out that Kris had entertained one of the girls, he ordered him to the clap-clinic in town without more ado, saying he could be stranded at sea with some infection of the nether regions and nobody could help him; Kris left the ship for the health centre.

We met for a drink in the city later and visited the unemployment office so that Kris could sign off and sail with us to the North Sea. We wandered from booth to booth looking for some help, but found ourselves being shunted from pillar to post. There were direction signs scattered about everywhere but they appeared to be of little use. Then I saw a sign which asked patrons of the building to deter from 'fighting or spitting.'

I thought that this was such a funny instruction, I took a photograph of it and was promptly marched away by two policemen into an outer office where I was questioned for an hour as to my intent. It appeared to be against the law to take pictures inside government buildings and with the problems in Ireland at the time, the police were a little edgy about an Englishman with a camera taking photographs. My film and camera were taken from me and I was marched off the premises with a stern warning not to commit such an offence again. I still thought the sign was humorous.

We were getting near the time when shipments of electrical parts were due to arrive from America and on checking the itinerary, it was noticed that a large alternator had been omitted from the checklist.

We could find no similar model in Dublin, so the quickest solution was to go directly to a manufacturer. I would have to hire a van and take the ferry from Rosslare to Cherbourg, drive up into Belgium, collect the equipment and then repeat the journey back to Dublin. I wanted Kris to come with me but this was not allowed, so I duly set off in my hired van early next morning, heading out of Dublin, past Christ Church Cathedral and following the road south that brought me to the ferry port of Rosslare.

CHAPTER 20

It was a fairly long drive south to the port, which took about three hours. I was on the ferry within another hour and shortly we were turning south and out into the Irish Channel. This trip was a darn sight better than the one I had made on the Magda Maria several months earlier. I headed for the bar and settled down with my drink and some newspapers in the viewing bay on the upper deck.

There was plenty to see as I walked around the ship a little later, and I soon became friendly with a young American fellow about my age who was backpacking around Europe, before going back to the States at the end of the summer to start college. His name was Joshua and he hitched a ride with me when we got to Cherburg; the drive to Belgium was so much more pleasurable with some company to while away the hours.

Joshua was from Rhode Island and he'd had a stormy relationship with his parents. It was decided it would be better for all concerned if he went away for the summer rather than stay at home and to that end, when we arrived in Belgium, he duly set off on his travels and I collected the alternator.

Shortly after my return to Dublin, the large container lorry with the transmitters and other equipment arrived from America. The transmitters were in large wooden crates which were cracked open on the dockside and lifted into the hold of the ship. The services of a Dutch engineer called José van Groningen were to be used in the installation of the new gear and he would travel back to the North Sea with us to set it all up. Years earlier, José had been the senior transmitter engineer on Radio Veronica and had now been employed by the Paradise team.

The plan was to run Radio Paradise on one of the two ten kilowatt medium wave transmitters twenty-four hours a day and the other one would be used for another Dutch language station to be called Radio Monique. Overnight, this frequency would be used for a new English radio station or maybe offered to Radio Caroline, depending on its situation. I was, at the time, out of touch with my former employers and although I knew of their new radioship, I had no idea as to its progress.

The Radio Paradise ship was to be anchored off the coast of England in the position formally occupied by the Mi Amigo the year before; it was deemed the safer option. The other possible plan had been to put the ship off the Dutch coast but this situation had never been tested since the introduction of the Dutch Marine Offences Act in nineteen seventy-four.

Work continued at quite a pace and José set about installing the transmitters whilst final preparations were completed with a mast company in Dublin to supply and fit the transmitting tower. Test transmission tapes were recorded in Dublin using the output of one of the new land-based pirate stations, Radio Nova. This was a station run by former Caroline deejay, Chris Carey, and was proving to be very successful. Another success story in Ireland was Sunshine Radio, this time run by another former Caroline deejay, Robbie Dale.

Several of my former colleagues from Caroline were working on these stations, oblivious to the fact there was an offshore radio station being fitted out on the Liffey. As long as the mast remained unseen, we hoped the whole project would remain secret. But rumours soon reached us that the authorities had been made aware of our presence and were showing an interest; we made plans to shrink the remaining work into a few days.

We all enjoyed another night in the pub and even Ben seemed relaxed considering the pressure that was on us to leave Ireland. We sat around a large circular table and talked of the expectations we had for the future.

It was not long before I found myself the in the spotlight, as one particular young girl in the pub made it very clear she was interested in me. Sitting down uninvited at our table, she joined in the conversation and made friends with the others who were egging me on to take things further. Her name was Maria and she was a pretty girl with a keen sense of humour and a pleasant Irish accent. She wore a smart frock and red shoes and had her hair tied back in a ponytail.

Maria came back to the ship with us and as we sat in the messroom having a drink, I tried to make it clear I was not particularly interested. But she still came and sat on my lap and kissed me, despite my protestations. The whole business proved to be very difficult, and I eventually managed to wangle my way out of the situation on some pretence and went downstairs to bed.

Half an hour later, I found myself hauled out of my bunk by a furious and pretty drunken Ben, dragged back upstairs by the scruff of my neck and made to explain why I had been encouraging this girl and then discarding her.

I was thrown into a chair upstairs in the messroom whilst Ben and José stood over me, resembling a couple of Nazi interrogators. Strangely, Maria had left her address onboard in case I should change my mind and had left the ship in floods of tears. This resulted in me being frog-marched off the ship by José and into a taxi. Next stop was Maria's house where I was made to knock at the door and ask a rather bemused man, whom I can only assume was her father, whether I could talk to Maria. She appeared without being summoned and I apologised to her for my alleged bad behaviour. She shrugged a sort of acknowledgment and walked away from me, back into the house. José said my treatment of this girl was appalling and he could not stand by whilst I behaved in this ill-mannered way. More embarrassment had been heaped upon me for a situation I did not encourage and the event caused intense ill-feeling between me and the two Radio Paradise men for several days. Nevertheless, I did often wonder why a young girl would be hanging around the docks area of a large city late at night, venturing into bars and chatting up strangers. Despite the problems, I think I had a lucky escape.

In time, the mast-men arrived in the form of Sammy Prendergast and his boys. They had installed several aerial systems across Ireland for the ever growing number of land-based pirate stations; but we were quite unacquainted with their abilities. The plan was to erect the mast in harbour and then, to save time, put the stays in place once the ship was underway. This idea caused me to voice an objection. Even though I now hated this whole project and several of the people involved, I still wanted it to succeed.

'It will come down in the Irish Sea if it remains without stays!' I protested. 'I do know something about this!' All to no avail, and once the pilot was onboard, the conversation ended.

It was now time to leave Dublin; the ropes were untied and after nearly four months of seriously hard work and emotional hell, we headed down the Liffey and out into the Irish Sea.

Kris had run out of cigarettes and there had been no time to run to the pub for more, as things had been moving too fast in those last few hours. He did not seem bothered though, and I wondered why as I watched him tidying up the ropes and stacking wooden crates safely away for our journey.

There was much more movement now and the ship rolled and pitched in the swell as I stood on the back deck watching the mast. I was ordered inside to make tea for the pilot and obeyed the 'fuehrer' Ben, but at my own speed. I went back to the galley to make myself some food and then made my way downstairs to find Kris smoking furiously in our cabin. He had broken into the bonded stores and helped himself. 'Well done, old fellow,' I remarked with some glee, and joined him on the bunk.

He told me he had been into the stores on more than one occasion, since the room had been sealed, by using a hatchway under the sink in the galley. We started laughing at this as Ben was not as clever as he thought, and at last someone had managed to get away with something, albeit small.

We went back up to the deck after a while and although it was not rough, the ship was still rolling heavily as we headed out to sea. Looking back towards land, I saw the twin towers of the power station taking on the appearance of painted matchsticks as they became just distant memories.

Suddenly, as we chatted, we heard a loud crack and looked up in time to see the top three sections tear from the top of the mast and fall into the sea, just avoiding the deck; that was sixty feet of our mast gone. The aerial riggers were still inside the ship and obviously heard nothing, so I beckoned Kris to follow me and we went to break the news.

The pilot boat came out to us to collect the pilot as soon as we reached open water and then we were on our own. It would take a couple of days to reach the English anchorage and I joined the others on the bridge to join in discussions about the shortened mast and the new anchorage.

CHAPTER 21

Next morning, a feeling of some success filtered through the ship and I sat down in the messroom to have breakfast. The remainder of the mast had now been stayed, and the transmitters would be ready for the big switch on once we had dropped anchor off Essex and made ourselves secure. A tender was on stand-by to come out to us when we located the anchorage and with a crew change completed, the test transmissions would begin.

But the biggest mistake of the Radio Paradise project was about to be made. Whether or not it was a decision made on the spur of the moment, I never did discover; maybe the plan was always lurking away in the recesses of Ben's brain. We headed away from the UK coast and out across the North Sea to take up our anchorage off the Dutch coast. It was the final, fatal mistake. Upon our arrival, the tender, the Bischon from Scheveningen, did indeed come alongside and I left the ship and went home to England for a week's shore leave. That was on Thursday afternoon and later that day, the tapes recorded in Ireland from Radio Nova were played. They were the first and last broadcasts to radiate from the Radio Paradise ship.

Reception was not good away from the local area and in England the signal was pretty inaudible. The mast was now far too short and propagation problems were a headache for José who had planned for a tower of much greater height.

I was still in bed at home when a lunchtime phone call woke me up and still sleepy from a fairly late night, I answered the call. It was Ben calling from Holland and he wasted no time in telling me the ship had been arrested at sea and was now on its way inland with the Dutch navy and police. He said he would call with more news later; I never heard from him again as it became clear the Radio Paradise project was over. The Dutch authorities had ambushed this offshore venture and nipped it in the bud.

My feelings were of total pain and anguish. The whole business had been fraught with difficulties and very hard work. There had been intense problems to overcome and the work and arguments had been excruciating at times. But to have it all snatched away like this was too much. I thought about poor Kris, maybe on his way to jail, for I had no idea how the Dutch courts would react if prosecutions were to take place. I had no contact with him again after that, but I have to hope he was okay.

There was nothing I could do now except get on with my life and try to earn a living. Radio Paradise took the Dutch government to court in a case that took seven years to be resolved. Our team won and the courts ordered that all equipment and the ship should be handed back; but by then it was too late. The ship had been vandalised in harbour and was now a wreck, whilst the organisation itself had disbanded with two of the financial backers having died by the time the case was resolved.

The courts declared it to be an illegal raid and it should never have happened. But it was not the first time the Dutch had acted in this way. For back in nineteen 1964, a raid was carried out on a radio and television station installed on a man-made island off the Dutch coast. The REM Island had been boarded in international waters and silenced. History had repeated itself seventeen years later.

Were the P a r a d i s e ship to have anchored off the English coast, all may have been well; I can only speculate. Plans for Radio Paradise to operate two radio stations including FM were far too ambitious in my opinion, and perhaps a single frequency from the p o l i t i c a l l y safer English coast may have tested the waters in the early days.

It's very easy with hindsight to criticise, but it could have turned out so differently.

CHAPTER 22

Things were moving fast in Santander, Spain, where the new Radio Caroline ship was being fitted out. I knew that former colleagues Peter Chicago and Tom Anderson were working on the ship, the Ross Revenge, but I felt no real interest to be involved in these early stages after what I had been through in Dublin. I was quite happy to let them work on and see what happened upon completion.

Radio Caroline had far better luck with their project than the unfortunate Paradise venture.

The Daily Mail had an aerial photograph of the ship making her way towards England across the Bay of Biscay, which must have caused a few heads to spin in Whitehall. It was nineteen eighty-three and it seemed as if Radio Caroline was on her way back, three and a half years after the Mi Amigo was lost in a storm.

The new ship was due on the air on the nineteenth of August and was to be anchored in the Knock Deep area of the North Sea, formally occupied by the m.v. Mi Amigo. The Ross Revenge was a thousand tonne former fishing trawler, and probably the best equipped radioship ever to anchor on the high seas.

She was featured on ITN's *News at Ten* having arrived at her anchorage and she looked serene and defiant sitting on the calm waters with her founder, Ronan O'Rahilly, interviewed on deck. He still had a twinkle in his eye and was as enthused as anyone could be about the station's future.

A line-up of presenters had been chosen and whatever discussions had taken place concerning the music format, the station came on the air sounding a little unsure as to what it should be doing. However, a feeling of euphoria overwhelmed me on hearing the first transmissions; nobody had ever believed Caroline could make it back on a brand new ship. A ship of such size and transmitter power.

I still felt very punch drunk about offshore radio and it was to be another nine months before I took the plunge and Stuart Russell appeared again on Radio Caroline.

July, nineteen eighty four, and I was in Ramsgate awaiting my first trip to the Ross Revenge. It was during the miner's strike and the dockside was awash with police. They were so preoccupied with pickets and possible trouble concerning the striking miners that we assumed we could walk along the harbour wall and get onto the tender without any problem.

But it was not to be and when we were stopped by the police, it oddly had nothing to do with Radio Caroline.

I had run to the newsagents across the road before they closed for lunch and bought a copy of each of the newspapers still on sale.

The policeman wanted to know what editions I had with me. 'Let's have a look there, please,' he said walking over to me. The other people in my company walked on as the policeman thumbed through the front pages of my newspapers. 'Well, no problem here.' He returned the papers and I joined the others at the end of the jetty.

It was not until later I realised exactly what he was seeking; left-wing newspapers supporting the miner's strike, which may have singled me out as a sympathiser. Luckily, the paper shop only had the Daily Mail, the Telegraph and the Sun; not exactly a hot bed of red flag-flying newsprint there, I mused. That was a lucky occurrence, because I would have bought the other papers had they been there, causing possible further questioning before I had even boarded the tender, something I did not necessitate.

Our tender was a good size and I was pleased things appeared to be so much better since my last involvement with Radio Caroline several years before. This station was still a magical entity to me and flowed through my veins, so it was good to be going back home.

The journey out into the North Sea was uneventful, thankfully, and I was becoming more and more excited at the prospect of seeing the new radioship. When she came into view, she was so red, so clean and so sleek with a three hundred foot radio mast streaking up into the light blue sky. She was magnificent beyond belief. This was the offshore radio station to end all offshore stations and I regretted not coming out to the ship earlier.

By now, we had competition on the high seas. Laser 558 was anchored a few miles away from Caroline and the government's attitude was hardening. This new station was an Irish backed setup, said to be born out of disputes with Ronan whilst they worked together in Spain on the Ross Revenge. Certain personnel had left the Caroline organisation and set up their own broadcasting venture.

Laser led a chequered life at sea with numerous problems, least of all several mast collapses and long periods off the air. She also possessed a ship, the Communicator, far smaller than Caroline's vessel and thus she suffered greatly in the North Sea storms.

The Ross Revenge was a beauty; I was in awe of her and loved her immediately. Stepping on board and hearing music coming from the open studio window was heart-stopping and I could not wait to go on the grand tour. I felt like an anorak on a hurried visit and had to pinch myself to remember I was Stuart Russell, who was due on the air in a couple of hours.

'The boat is leaving now, anyone going ashore please hurry up!' came the captain's announcement from above. The captain, an Englishman from Kent called Mick, barked these orders from the upper deck and then came down the ladder to join us below. He was from Minster on the Isle of Sheppey, a place I knew well and we soon found we had several things in common. He was well versed with Sheerness and may have even known my father as he used to work on the pilot cutters and got to know many of the pilots.

This ship seemed to be a pirate's dream; she was full of fuel and water and had food to last for months. Morale was high, life was good and there was no sign of any serious government intervention so far.

The Ross Revenge was two hundred and twenty-two feet long and thirty-eight feet wide. Formerly known as the m.v. Freyr, she was built in nineteen sixty and given an ice strengthened hull due to her work as an Icelandic fishing trawler. Later sold to Ross Trawlers, she had her name changed to the Ross Revenge in 1963 and gained a new registration number, GY718.

Her broadcasting capabilities were an RCA fifty kilowatt AM from Canada, a ten kilowatt AM transmitter manufactured by RCA in North America and a five kilowatt, which after much work, became a ten kilowatt shortwave unit.

My first show on Caroline's new ship was not as nerve wracking as the first one on the Mi Amigo. This time I did not shake with terror as I tried to cue up records and knew not to tell the time two times a link. I hoped I had learned a few things during my short time in broadcasting.

It occurred to me that this was my fourth radioship, although only the second one that had actually made it onto the air. Both times it had been with Radio Caroline so it seemed we ruled the offshore airwaves and woe betide anyone else who tried to install themselves on our territory, even Laser.

The weather remained remarkably good that early summer and Caroline and Laser 558 continued to broadcast in the sunshine but there seemed to be a dispute of sorts between the two ships by the time I arrived.

Crispian St John, a former Caroline, Radio North Sea and Atlantis deejay, who this time called himself Jay Jackson and was head of news on Caroline, had forbidden anyone going over to the Laser ship in the rubberboat, although in past months this had been a regular occurrence with teams from both ships making visits to see each other. The captain refused to say anything on the matter and the visits had been suspended. I never fully understood the nature of the dispute, but I gambled there was a fair chance a woman was involved in the trouble.

Some years later, Jay Jackson went on to run a trade paper for the radio industry, the 'Radio Magazine', this time under his real name, Howard Rose. Unfortunately, he died from complications following surgery in 2002.

Sometimes, it was easy to forget about the bad periods I had suffered on the Mi Amigo because this time, nothing seemed to go wrong. We had an English station on the air twenty-four hours a day, something that had not happened in a long while, and at a time when very few radio stations in the UK were on the air round-the-clock.

We had millions of listeners and the signal was strong and stable. Tenders continued to arrive on schedule and we always had plenty of supplies; it seemed nothing could ever go wrong.

Amongst our crew on that trip to the Ross Revenge was Mike from the office; an easy-going chap and good company. Along with him, we had an American, Blake Williams, who had joined Caroline from Laser 558. Sadly, he only did one stint on Caroline and left Europe to work on forces radio in Guam. Engineering was the domain of Stuart Vincent, who moved across to Laser within a few months.

My month on board soon ran out and I left on the tender for England. Having enjoyed myself so much, I was sad to leave but one problem remained whilst working for Radio Caroline; there was no money. I needed money to live even though I was still at home, with mum asking for little or no money from me for the privilege.

I had debts building up and they needed to be addressed at some point, so with this in mind, I got a driving job which lasted until autumn, nineteen eighty-seven.

I had acquired a new position of sub-organist at the main parish church of St. Michael in Sittingbourne shortly before my nineteen eight-four return to Caroline, and any time at sea would have to be finely balanced with my new duties. Future shore leaves would be taken up with a completely different kind of music; hymns, psalms, anthems and powerful organ works replaced Led Zeppelin and the Electric Light Orchestra.

Continued organ lessons became a regular event too, and thus any time spent on land was always busy. Several visits to Rochester Cathedral with the church choir also took place requiring an incredible amount of practice and steady nerves, as the cathedral organ was large and extremely powerful.

Whilst I was on shore, Laser 558 had gone off the air due to government pressure and heavy surveillance of both ships, dubbed 'Eurosiege'. The station had been relaunched a little later as Laser Hot Hits but lack of money and bad management caused the new project to founder and she succumbed once more.

For me, the pull to go back to sea was too strong to resist any longer. A station called Radio Monique, the same one that was due to join Radio Paradise in nineteen eighty-one, had now taken the daytime hours on Radio Caroline and was providing much needed income to run the ship.

I was due to go back to the ship in October, nineteen eighty-seven but bad weather prevented that trip and whilst waiting to return to the Ross Revenge, she suffered the full fury of the great hurricane. Radio Caroline remained on the air, despite the appalling conditions at sea, far longer than many land-based rivals. Caroline presenter, Peter Phillips, on the air during the hurricane, famously described the conditions outside his studio window as a 'seething cauldron of saline hostility!'

The Ross Revenge escaped from that nightmare and I made my trip into the North Sea a short while later to find the ship battered and bruised, but in one piece. Some of the people on board wanted to get off and swore they would never set foot on the ship again. It must have been an horrific experience and one I hoped I would never have to endure.

CHAPTER 23

It was now November and the winter storms were gathering. Since my last visit, the Ross Revenge had moved from her original anchorage in the Knock Deep off the Essex coast, to an area about eighteen miles northeast of Margate, known as the Fall's Head. The British government had redrawn the territorial limits to include the area where the Ross Revenge had previously been moored. She was now anchored in an area of water that even hardened seafarers thought of as difficult; it was where several currents met and the seas could be very confused and rough at times, with no protection afforded from any sandbanks.

Peter Philips was our programme controller onboard at the time and he was due to go on shore leave which would leave Kevin Turner as our senior presenter. Peter had brought to Caroline a pop service which had held on to millions of listeners on the five-five-eight frequency when vacated by Laser.

Caroline now had a tight format system which stabilised the sound of the station. It was not entirely to my liking but I like to think that I can adapt to any situation and after all, Caroline had re-hired me and it was not up to me to complain about the music as soon as I arrived onboard.

There were some, however, who could not wait to see the back of Peter and thus change the station output; many plots were stirring to that end. However, events would soon take over and Peter Philips would leave of his own accord.

The team onboard towards the end of nineteen eighty-seven were a good bunch including Tim Allen, Pat Brooks, Keith Francis and a globe-trotting New Zealander. Tim and our Kiwi friend had been traumatised by the hurricane but had been brave enough to stay on the boat when it was asked of them, even though they were given the chance of going ashore.

This time on Caroline, I had a different name and was to be known as Nigel Harris. I changed to avoid confusion; so many times I had been called 'Nigel' on the air, my real Christian name, to be followed closely by, 'Oh sorry, I mean Stuart'.

Peter Philips left a week later for shore leave and we got on with the job of running the two radio stations twenty-four hours a day. Caroline was now on the air round-the-clock on one frequency whilst Radio Monique remained on the air until seven at night on another channel, with

Caroline's religious programming and a format of album tracks taking over through the night, with programming under the 'Caroline Overdrive' banner.

Yet another station was soon to appear on the Ross Revenge and would be known as World Mission Radio. It was an American religious station with pre-recorded tapes and was run using the transmitter earlier converted to shortwave. We spent a day off the air so the aerial could be installed high up in the three hundred foot mast. If the engineer, Mike Watts who made the climb, had been aware of what was to happen days later, he certainly would not have gone up the tower.

One afternoon late in November, I filmed fellow presenter, Pat Brooks, as he played around on the forepeak in the strengthening winds. In the distance I spotted one of the two Olau ferries that plied the North Sea between Sheerness and Vlissingen in Holland. Onboard this ferry was a friend from my church, Ian, who knowing I was on the ship, took what were to be the last photographs of the Ross Revenge in her current state. He needed his telephoto lens this windy afternoon as when the seas were rough, the ferries always kept a greater distance from the radioship, whilst calmer waters brought the two vessels closer together.

Today it was getting rougher by the hour and as I peered through the studio porthole during my teatime show, I watched the fishing boats running for cover. It was late afternoon and getting quite dark as the smell of dinner drifted through the ship. Dinnertime was the occasion of the great gathering when all forces from within the ship met, ate, discussed and hopefully sorted out any differences.

Being forced together like this usually meant that bad moods, grievances and general problems acquired during the day could be sorted out. There was no hiding from the other party and feelings had to be really dire for arguments to last very long. On this day, everybody was being friendly and as six o'clock drew closer, I looked forward to dinner and some television afterwards.

It was one of those meals when the storm-breaks had been put in place. These were a criss-cross of wooden bars locked into a series of squares across the messroom table thus holding plates and bowls in place rather than allowing them to slide inevitably into one's lap. *(See picture, lower, page 136)*

It had been a troublesome afternoon in the galley with pots, pans and plates rolling and crashing randomly around as our cook tried to hold things steady. All was now prepared and we gathered around the dinner table, beers in hand. We ate well that night, which was lucky, as it was not to happen again for quite a while. Ernie Stevenson was our captain and chief diesel engineer. He was a former officer on the Ross Revenge when she was part of the Ross fishing fleet, and he relished being back on his old ship. He was a kindly man with a gruff spirit and a stickler for good manners. The ship always came before the radio station and on several occasions, he was known to badger a poor deejay out of the studio to attend to some ship's business.

By about nine o'clock, the seas were so rough that furniture was moving of its own accord and in the studio, carts were flying out of the racks, as the records skipped time and time again. In the messroom, a really steep roll had caused the settee and its four occupants to fly across the room and into the opposite wall, as if projected by a poltergeist.

We all laughed and screamed in excitement, ignoring the severity of the situation, whilst waiting for it to happen again. Some had taken to their beds for solace whilst others clung on for dear life to whatever part of the ship they happened to find themselves. I was never one for bed in a storm as I could not sleep and I needed to know what was going on, for in the event of a capsize situation, the last place I wanted to be was below decks.

The weather got worse as the evening wore on and by midnight things were so bad that one of the feeder cables that ran up from the base of the three hundred foot mast had torn itself free from the top, causing considerable electrical arcing. Our broadcast engineer, Peter Chicago, turned off the transmitters.

The ship was taking on such obscene angles as she rolled from side to side, we began to think the anchor chain had broken, but our Decca navigator on the bridge showed us we were securely on station. It was very unusual to roll over to such degrees but these discrepancies did not concern us at the time and I went below to get my video camera to film the goings on; I wanted to keep these bizarre memories forever.

It was a struggle to get below deck and I found my cabin almost destroyed by the storm. Fittings had come away from the wall and the wooden slats on the base of the bunk had been torn up and now lay across the floor; the only thing still in its place seemed to be the sink. I grabbed my camera from amongst a mass of clothing and clawed my way up two levels of the ship, past the studio and into the record library. Some individuals were having a whale of a time in there as others suffered from sickness and sheer fright below in their bunks. I felt sorry for those who suffered during this storm but there was little anyone could do; it would be over soon and everything would be alright again.

All we had to do was sit it out for another few hours, and then go and get some sleep. Peter Chicago was in his cabin above us, wandering out onto the bridge at regular intervals to keep an eye on things. Captain Ernie was in the messroom, and so we imagined all angles were covered. We could have a laugh in the roller-coaster that was our ship as she played in the rough seas. She played hard that night and I ran up onto the bridge to peer out into the darkness at the mountainous seas as they threw us around like an uprooted tree in a tornado.

The storm was relentless and went on hour after hour, steadily increasing in its ferociousness. I stared out through the bridge windows, squinting into the darkness, trying to make out a shape of some sort, something, anything from which to get a bearing. But there was nothing but dark black sea, and a lot of spray, lit ominously by our powerful arc lamps. They continued to shine out across the decks and into the night sky.

I clambered back down into the record library where some were still gathered, including Tim Allen, who was having great fun getting thrown around. I was pleased to see him not fretting too much after the horrors of the hurricane a few weeks earlier.

Now it was time to get some pictures and I turned on the camera just as Tim and Pat went flying across the library in fits of laughter with me in close pursuit. Expletives seemed to echo from every direction as bodies collided from all sides.

Suddenly the ship appeared almost motionless after a steep roll to port. She appeared to freeze in mid-air as if in space. We looked at each other, our faces perplexed and our voices now silent. An almighty crash ended this short lived nirvana and Tim said, almost casually, 'What the fuck's that?' I replied, just as matter-of-factly, 'Don't worry, it's only stuff on the bridge.' What none of us realised in those first few seconds was this sentence was in fact very true; stuff was on the bridge, literally. It was huge sections of our mast as all three hundred feet of it came crashing down onto the ship as she battled the almighty storm far out in the North Sea. 'The mast, it's down!' I shrieked as we headed with all haste for the door and lower decks.

Those below in their cabins had come up on hearing the almighty crashing sounds which were still going on outside as stays snapped, insulators shattered and metalwork was pulled from all parts of the vessel.

Alarm bells sounded throughout the ship as people gathered along the corridors on the main deck level. Captain Ernie ordered us to put on lifejackets and in the initial rush, there appeared to be too few to go round, causing panic amongst those who did not possess one. I gave mine to an ashen faced Dutch fellow, who in the initial panic now enveloping the ship, had started to cry hysterically. Captain Ernie managed to comfort him, explaining that everything would be alright. I wandered about with my camera still running but tightly gripped at arm's length. It was not fair to keep pointing it at people in distress; naturally, some of the crew were very frightened, including me.

We had suffered some severe rolling earlier in the night but now, without the stability our mast afforded, we rolled with an increased intensity. On one occasion, the ship went over to forty-five degrees. Our centre of gravity had changed and some thought we would actually roll over. The captain swiftly assured us of our safety. He said he had been through far worse on this very same ship some years earlier while fishing in the Arctic. 'This vessel can handle much worse!' he shouted above the chaos of noise from the storm outside. He looked into the petrified faces of those around him and added, 'We'll all have some tea when I have discussed the situation with the engineers.'

I would be lying to say I was not scared, but I had been through some pretty severe storms in my time at sea on a far smaller ship than this one. I still had confidence in the Ross Revenge but felt desperate at the situation.

We were forbidden to go outside, so it was not until first light that we could see the full damage of the night before. The entire three hundred foot mast had collapsed. All that remained were a few inches of twisted metal in each of the three corners of the base around the shattered porcelain insulator.

CHAPTER 24

The crew stood on the bridge, some with mugs of hot tea held close for extra warmth. We all stretched our gaze out onto the deck below, where Captain Ernie and Peter Chicago were cutting off the remaining parts of our mast and stays with oxyacetylene equipment. Sparks flew everywhere in the wind and although the seas had eased a little, it was still atrociously rough. The Olau ferry was steaming past, again many miles away from the ship, and we must have looked a strange sight without our familiar three hundred foot mast swaying in the sky, high above the radioship.

We had no contact with our offices on land, either in Holland or England, but we were in touch with the coastguard who assured us they were keeping an eye on the situation. We stressed that we were in no immediate danger, but that conditions remained difficult.

It had been a culmination of events that caused this latest catastrophe. A month earlier, the ship had been through the worst storm to hit the southeast of England in hundreds of years. The great hurricane had truly weakened the mast and it had taken a battering that even a tower on land would have found hard to resist. The fact it did not come down during the hurricane was testament to the expertise of the riggers in Spain.

Since it was installed, maintenance on the mast had become haphazard and then virtually non existent; the stays had not been checked and tightened for a considerable length of time. This had allowed the mast to move more than it should on the night of the hurricane as the ship pitched into the heavy seas, hour after hour.

The storm that brought down the mast was different in that the wind direction and speed varied throughout the course of the two days before it fell. Then the night it collapsed, the ship had been rolling from side to side for many hours, sometimes corkscrewing in the swirling seas, thus putting strain on different sections of the mast and substantially weakening the structure at the base, which resulted in cataclysmic failure. An element of metal fatigue was already a feature and the combination of these factors met in one place on that dreadful night.

Ronan, on hearing the news, assumed the very top section had fallen off, maybe twenty feet at most, and that broadcasting could continue unaffected when repairs had been undertaken.

It was almost a week before w e saw a tender from England. Those onboard the visiting boat had come out on an inspection mission rather than to offer any real assistance, and were soon on their way home again, leaving one extra man on the Ross Revenge. This was Tony Peters who decided that for morale purposes, we should resume our programmes even though we were not on the air. His sentiments may have been well intended but were met with total derision by the presenters.

However, Tony was to come to my rescue days later. Cleaning up the deck of the ship was an important task after the storm and a large chunk of the former insulator was to be discarded over the side. As several of us balanced this huge slice of jagged porcelain on the side of the ship, ready to let go and release it into the choppy seas, it flipped back as the ship rolled, and as it fell into the water below, a sharp edge caught me on the wrist, tearing my flesh open.

I appealed to Chicago for help, but alas, the sight of blood is something he cannot tolerate. The blood was spurting four or five inches out and I was beginning to seriously panic. Tony had worked at Sheppey General Hospital in previous years and he had me sutured and bandaged up in no time, which was a blessèd relief.

The decision to resume broadcasting as soon as we could was an easy one to make and we thought the best idea was to get some semblance of aerial erected. Being short of parts, improvisation with odds and ends found around the ship was the only way to proceed.

An aerial array was strung between the top of the ship's own rather stumpy mast at the front, across the deck and back to the bridge where we had erected what was no more than a short pole. Insulators were installed and one of the smaller transmitters fired up on very low power. A limited amount of radiation was all the temporary aerial could afford before bursting into flames.

It was not until later we discovered our signal barely reached Margate beach and after dark, the signal was inaudible; but it was a start.

As a former fishing vessel, the Ross Revenge still possessed a certain amount of gear from those days spent in the Arctic. A few hundred feet of pipe, used to carry the cod liver oil and other fish innards away whilst at sea, was still onboard and work went on in earnest to turn some of this pipe-work into a front mast. Peter Phillips returned to help design this new mast and Mike Watts, our second engineer, cut the pipes to length for the task. The smell of cod liver oil and fish-guts hung about the ship for weeks.

In time, the new system was installed and the two stations were able to broadcast again. However by now, the Radio Monique organisation had ceased to function and a new Dutch partner was found for daytime broadcasting.

We had a good sized front mast now with the fish-gut pipe and a crank-up mast was sent out to be used as the back mast. Still unable to run at full power, the new mast system was able to give us a reasonable signal that covered a good part of Europe and things soon settled into as near a normal pattern as could be expected under the circumstances.

The radio station struggled to make enough money to stay on the air and, as with the Mi Amigo, repairs and general maintenance were repeatedly neglected.

A man I had met almost ten years ago now started to have more to do with Radio Caroline. The English organisation had all but disappeared and Peter Moore had been sanctioned by Ronan to help things function at sea.

I thought of Peter as a friend and spent many hours in the secret Highgate office whilst on leave, waiting to go to the pub after Peter finished work at his carburettor shop. There, we would discuss plans for the tenders and what we could afford to buy for the station with the very little money we possessed.

Captain Ernie was still with us, although he was now getting on in years. He still loved the concept of Radio Caroline and was excited everytime he stepped onto his beloved ship, the Ross Revenge.

We saw a huge turnover of presenters at Radio Caroline in those latter years and with so many local stations to choose from on land, it became much more of a stepping stone to a job somewhere in the UK radio market for some. Our continuity suffered as very few presenters came back for more than a couple of trips at most, and although the situation on board provided them with food, fags and booze, there was no salary of any kind to entice them back.

At home one afternoon, I was watching some videos I had taken on the ship and suddenly came up with the idea of selling copies of the video I made on the night the three hundred foot mast came down.

I edited some five hours down to an hour, put some captions and a little commentary on the tape and soon we had an advertisement for the video running on the radio station. The tape was a little amateurish to say the least, as home video technology was not very advanced in the eighties, but it gave an interesting insight into activities on the ship during the disaster.

I opened a box number in London with a company that swore total secrecy and discretion; they said they would not divulge the client's name or address under any circumstances, so this seemed ideal for our sales company. I had no bank account of my own so my mum opened one for me in her name and we called the new company 'Solar Video'.

The hope was that people would buy the tape and we could pay the deejays a salary, a meagre one maybe, but something to encourage them to stay with Caroline.

It became a full time job getting the tapes copied and posted to places all over Europe. Everytime the postman came to the house, there were bundles of orders forwarded from the box number in London. It was anybody's guess how long we would get away with this, but due to the appalling state of Caroline's finances, all the money now went towards English tenders and extra food for the boat.

As nineteen eighty-nine moved into the summer months, things were again starting to look up, if ever so slightly, for our troubled organisation. A new professional front mast had been completed using sections smuggled out from the English coast and driven along country lanes barely wide enough to cope, on the open top of a double-decker bus owned by a good friend of Radio Caroline, John Burch.

One double section of the first tier of back mast had been welded to the deck and we were waiting for the rigger-team to reappear later in the month to carry on the work. Things, at last, were beginning to move forward, and the team onboard was filled with a new level of confidence.

CHAPTER 25

Radio Caroline celebrated her twenty-fifth birthday in March, nineteen eighty-nine, and a ferry trip to Holland onboard the Olau ferry was organised. I got a lift to Sheerness port with my mother and took with me dozens of t-shirts and videos to sell to the excited fans onboard. All those on shore leave came along, including our founder Ronan O'Rahilly and several of our tender skippers. There were hundreds of listeners with us and it must have been one of the ferry's busiest runs.

Organising the special ferry crossing was not an easy task for the team, led by John Burch. The Department of Trade and Industry, now the office responsible for causing Caroline as much aggravation as possible, tried on numerous occasions to find ways of scuppering our weekend return voyage to Holland.

We were to pass the radioship on the journey out, but as it was late at night, we decided to leave the celebrations until the trip back when we would be able to see the ship a little more closely; the captain had promised us a close pass. In the meantime, we drank our fill with the fans in the ballroom and watched the cabaret with some apprehension. I had my video camera with me again and so spent a lot of the time shoving my lens into grinning faces with varying amounts of success. The turn around in Holland was quick and soon we were on our way back across the North Sea.

Sadly, a dense fog had descended in the area around the Ross Revenge, which made visibility a little difficult. Even with my camera's powerful zoom lens, it was not easy to make out shapes on board the radio station as we steamed past late that afternoon. Both vessels blasted their sirens at each other and we got a glimpse of the Ross Revenge through the swirling sea fog.

I sold all the merchandise I had taken with me, and on docking, headed out through customs in Sheerness, feeling quite pleased that the weekend had gone reasonably well. That is until I was pulled in for questioning by customs officers.

I could not believe it; Ronan had gone through unchallenged, along with Peter Moore and the many fans of Radio Caroline. Then I arrived on the scene.

'Sir, please, this way!' I was taken to the back of the hallway and told to sit down. Did I have anything to declare on my person? Did I make this trip on a regular basis? Did I spend long amounts of time outside the UK? There was no mention of Radio Caroline which I thought was odd, but why I was singled out from such a vast crowd was a mystery. Maybe they knew more than I thought they did. Or was it just coincidence? Within fifteen minutes, I was on my way to the car waiting in the high street.

Our spirits were lifted by a poll carried out by the music paper Record Mirror that month. A poll of reader's favourite stations had put Radio Caroline in third place, behind Radio One and London's Capital FM. We were also just ahead of Newcastle's Metro, Radio Four and Luxembourg; this potentially gave Caroline an audience of at least one million in the UK alone.

The Sunday Times wrote a 'Happy 25th Birthday' article in February of nineteen eighty-nine, wishing Caroline all the best for another twenty-five years. With these accolades ringing in our ears, we thought we had a promising future.

As the summer months continued to give us reasonably good weather, we managed to get a few more supply boats out to the ship with the extra money afforded us by sales of the video tapes. It seemed that the authorities were leaving us alone and we decided to increase our sales items to include t-shirts and stickers. The orders continued to arrive and our little team continued to dispatch them as quickly as possible.

Radio Caroline was still running with the pop music format devised by Peter Phillips and since his departure, there had been no permanent programme controller on the ship. Steve Conway took over the position for several stints onboard and held the station together. He, too, left for a while, to involve himself in other projects and the post was then occupied by a succession of people over the next few months.

It was decided that this must change, and after a meeting in London with Ronan O'Rahilly, I was offered the post, which I accepted. Many ideas were put forward as to the future sound of the station and meetings held with Peter Moore brought forth even more. We had Radio Caroline on the air twenty four hours a day on one frequency and an alternative service started after the day's Dutch programming had ceased, on a separate channel; religion was on yet another and as a consequence, there was a lot of airtime to fill.

Listening to the station whilst on land on Saturday morning, the twenty-second of July, nineteen eighty-nine, I was surprised to hear that code numbers were to be read out for the office after the next scheduled news bulletin. I dutifully sat by the radio, code list in hand, waiting and speculating. The weather was good, so it couldn't be too serious; that was my initial thought, at least.

But when I checked the numbers against my own, a horrible truth dawned on me. We had been going through the calm before the storm, for there was an English police boat, the Vigilant III, alongside the Ross Revenge ordering our tender to leave the vicinity of the radioship. It was a Belgian trawler delivering fuel, so how much had been pumped, if any, before the police arrived, was anybody's guess. In all my time with Caroline, I had never before experienced this kind of situation.

We set up a new list of codes that week to describe in more detail the situation in the area close to our ship. If we had a tender on the way, the last thing we needed was for it to sail into the arms of the law.

Over the next week or two, we saw the French Navy come close to the Ross Revenge and had several more visits from the British police. This was a giant headache for the office as we continued our attempts to supply the ship. We relied on our code list for windows of safety and would make a quick dash to the radioship if the coast appeared clear.

Our tender skipper at the time was a fisherman from Herne Bay with the moniker of Dave the Fish. He was a heavy metal music fan with a mad streak, a manic laugh and perfect for the job. Anyone with a modicum of intelligence would have run a mile from the Caroline organisation, but we were all tarred with the same brush, thus it went hand-in-hand that Dave would join us.

The penalties were severe for skippers caught supplying the ship and we needed more than just one boat for the services required. I went on yet another boat seeking mission and found someone willing to do the job with a boat moored in a small inlet near Richborough Power station on the southeast coast of England.

We would alternate these two boats and Peter Moore hoped to get a third vessel involved and so lessen the risk of being apprehended; or so we hoped at the time.

Later in the week, we were again on our way out to sea with supplies for the ship, including more equipment to help complete the mast building mission. 'Make sure we catch the codes in half an hour,' someone shouted from the wheelhouse. 'We don't want to sail into a trap.' The codes given on the air gave the all clear and we headed on towards the Ross Revenge through the clear blue sea, the like of which I had not seen in a long time; it gave the whole day a Mediterranean feel. We constantly scanned the horizon for any vessels lurking in our vicinity as we headed towards our target; we saw none that posed a threat.

Our boat was alongside the Ross Revenge within two hours and we got on with the task of unloading supplies as we did not want the tender alongside the ship for too long. We had a lookout on the roof of the bridge of the radioship, watching for approaching boats but all seemed fine, and our tender made a clean getaway back to England.

We possessed a mobile phone on the ship now which was used sparingly and only for emergencies. We were fully aware that the authorities could monitor any traffic from the ship to colleagues on land. Some people broke the rules to make personal calls, so it was adapted for incoming calls only, unless a secret code number was punched in first.

My appointment as programme controller on Radio Caroline caused some resentment and jealousy amongst a small number of people, including one man with whom I had been friends for several years.

Presenter Dave Richards appeared particularly unhappy with the situation and made his feelings clear when he approached me in the newsroom one evening.

'You are not the person who should be doing this, it should be me! You really have no idea what you are doing!' He carried on in a similar vein for a few minutes, whilst I sat and listened, feeling rather mystified at this sudden change of manner from someone I saw as a friend. Dave Richards left the room, refusing to have much more to do with me and from that evening, communicated with me via a third party, going out of his way to be difficult.

My immediate job was to overhaul the station's music policy and I decided that rather than change the sound of the station overnight, it would be better to make any changes gradually and not alienate the many listeners we had built up. As an initial move, I removed the Stock/Aitken/ Waterman songs and the top end pop that had been played so much over the previous years. I also reduced the number of sixties songs played in the daytime to bring a more up-to-date sound to the station. My next plan was to lessen the reliance on former chart material and introduce more album tracks into the system.

We had the alternative service on our second frequency at night, so other tastes were being catered for while changes were made on the main channel. My plan was to get all the changes through within the month and then do away with the tight format system, allowing the deejays to choose more tracks for themselves from a much looser structure of format. It had worked on the Mi Amigo and I saw no reason why it would not work on the Ross Revenge.

But petty arguments continued to take place about who should be in charge. My reply to those people was always the same. Go to London and see Ronan, let him know of any problems with me, and then he could decide what to do. Nobody ever went to see him.

It would be supercilious of me to say I did everything perfectly but the problems started on my first night back on the ship and I think I should have been allowed time to get my plans in motion before coming under such virulent attack.

Within a few days, there was a little less frostiness from Dave Richards towards me, as he probably realised he could not gain control of the station and there were changes being made to the format he appeared to dislike so much. Not at the speed he insisted, but he had certainly calmed down somewhat, which was a blessing as far as I was concerned.

We now had new advertisements being broadcast for our special summer range of merchandise, including more t-shirts and stickers. Word came from the land staff saying that orders were still coming in from our loyal listeners. Those buying our wares did not realise at the time how much they were helping the station, as money was running desperately short. To make matters worse, we were now getting reports that in France, Holland and Belgium, the police were starting yet another round of sudden crackdowns and some arrests had already been made.

CHAPTER 26

My show started at nine in the morning and I had occupied this slot since coming back to the ship two weeks earlier. It was August the eighteenth, nineteen eighty-nine and the summer sun shone strongly down on the Ross Revenge as she sat at anchor on the tranquil North Sea.

I first spotted the early morning visitor through the studio window which looked out towards the stern; it was a small vessel, slowly making its way towards us from the direction of the north Kent coast. I ran to the bridge and grabbed the binoculars from the wall mounting and peered across the water. It was definitely coming our way but was too far off yet to make out clearly. I jumped down the steps from the bridge to the studio below in a couple of large bounds and got back just in time as my record finished. I made no mention of the approaching boat on the air and continued as normal with my programme. Crewmembers had now gathered along the back deck of the radioship and were staring out to sea, wondering who could be coming to see us.

Within thirty minutes, the visiting boat was approaching our stern. It flew the Ensign on the stern flag-pole, so it was an official vessel as far as I could tell. I stayed inside the ship and away from prying eyes; the whole episode was continually filmed from the bows of the boat called the *Landward*.

I watched from the bridge as some of our team hung over the stern of the Ross Revenge talking to the visitors, and it wasn't until one of our party came back inside the ship that I realised the magnitude of the visit that warm Friday morning. It was a vessel under charter to the Department of Trade and Industry with responsibility to the Radio Communications Agency. I hoped it was just another example of sabre-rattling from the UK authorities to back up the occasional police visits.

My shift was soon over and we had still not reported the incident on the air, although we had recently received a message from the visiting boat which was sinister and brief. They informed us that our crew must evacuate the Ross Revenge and go back to the UK with them. When questioned as to the fate of the ship, they declined to answer. Our response to their request was naturally enough a negative one, and the vessel backed off. The Landward started to circle us, as a predator circles its prey.

It sailed round and round us for the next couple of hours, occasionally nudging us amidships, and then moving on again. One of our crew went on board the Landward for discussions with the DTI men and came back revealing very little that we did not already know.

I have my suspicions about this man, and I strongly believe he changed sides that day and volunteered a great deal of information about our organisation. He accepted cigarettes and drinks whilst on the Landward and seemed to be enjoying himself as he laughed and joked, taking on the role of unofficial Caroline spokesman.

This man came to the Ross Revenge on the recommendation of Dave Richards, with Peter Moore commenting later that it was against his better judgment to have allowed him onboard.

It was now lunchtime and for the first time that day, we made mention of the DTI's presence in our one o'clock news bulletin. Shortly afterwards, we got a call on the ship's cell phone from one of our agents on land; the situation was explained to him and he dutifully reported the facts to Peter Moore in London.

We had been told by the DTI that the entire organisation in England and on the continent had been arrested and we were now on our own. The only thing we could do was give up, surrender the ship and be taken back to England. However, a further call from our land team stated that nobody in England had been arrested, and our office would investigate the claims being made by the DTI concerning our continental colleagues.

Life onboard routinely continued despite our concerns, and I went below to pump some more fuel into the day tank that directly feeds the generators. Filling it to the maximum level so that I would not have to worry about it again for some time, I remembered that I had to switch generators later that night; an oil and filter change was long overdue on the generator that was currently in use.

Peter Chicago was on shore leave whilst all this was taking place and Captain Ernie had been away for some time due to illness, so I did my best with the transmitters and generators whilst hoping for a little bit of luck too. The DTI visit was causing us great anxiety and I thought long and hard about what they had in store for us now that we had failed to comply with their request to abandon our ship.

In the galley, I made myself a sandwich and went into the messroom, grabbing a beer from the fridge.

Dinner that night was the usual affair as we all crowded around the messroom table. It was still light and we could see the Landward pass by the portholes from time to time. The talk was about what we thought would happen next and a recent visit alongside for a bit of boat-nudging had brought a little more information from the DTI. The man on the bow had almost begged us at one point to give up and switch off the transmitters, saying if we did not do so, stage two of the operation would follow. Any further details about what this may have been were, as usual, not forthcoming.

Dinner over, we settled down to watch television while keeping an eye on the Landward. Shortly after nine o'clock, she was spotted dropping her anchor about a hundred yards off our port bow; we were to be kept under watch overnight.

The phone on the bridge rang a little later and I was surprised to hear from Peter Chicago. I explained the current situation and he wished us good luck and hung up, saying it was his dinnertime but he would be in touch later.

It was now time to switch generators, and there was a knack to keeping the power stable during the swap over that sometimes worked and sometimes not. I managed it this time by getting the second engine up to speed and then switching from the first generator to the second with no drop in current to the transmitters. Powering down the first engine, I bought it to a halt and headed back up the ladder to the deck and out into the late evening sunshine. The Landward was still wallowing off our port side and for the first time, I seriously began to wonder, as I stood there alone, whether this was really the end for Radio Caroline.

I went back below and carried out an oil and filter change on the overworked generator, my heart in my mouth the whole time.

Going back inside the ship, I went down to my cabin and lay on my bunk, exhausted after the day's events. It wasn't long before I got up again, my mind racing with all too many outcomes to this nightmare.

It was shortly before ten when I climbed up to the bridge and studied the Landward for the last time before going back to my cabin. There were men leaning over the bow, looking into the water; it was obvious they were having a problem of some sort. Suddenly, there was a splash just in front of their boat as smoke belched from the exhaust; the engines roared into life and the boat turned, heading for England.

We could only assume they were trying to raise the anchor and have another look round the Ross Revenge but found their chain had snagged somewhere, making it impossible to heave up. Dropping it to the bottom and returning to base was their only option.

At least they were gone for now and we even wondered, for a precious moment, if that would be the end of it all; it seemed unlikely, but we hoped.

I went back to bed, falling asleep within moments, my mind closing down to all the trouble we were encountering as we sat unaided on the high seas, unsure of the future.

Around five o'clock that morning I awoke, feeling thirsty and keen to see whether the DTI boat was back again. But I had the surprise of my life on walking into the galley. For a split second, I assumed I was hallucinating, for right infront of me, making breakfast, was Peter Chicago. I assumed we'd had a tender during the night. 'Why did nobody wake me?' I queried of those in the galley. 'When did the tender get here?' Peter said nothing, and nor did anyone else. I shrugged, poured myself some orange juice and went out on deck. There was no sign of the Landward or of any tender that may have been heading homeward having delivered Peter. I could not understand it as I always woke up when tenders arrived alongside our ship.

The truth was even more implausible than I could have imagined. Peter had left home in the early hours and headed for the beach with a one man rubberboat, an outboard motor, a lifejacket and a radio for direction finding. It had taken him many hours to reach the Ross Revenge, and alone on the North Sea at night in a boat designed for inshore waters or rivers at best, he had put his life at considerable risk. He had headed out across the busiest shipping lanes in the world to come to the aid of his friends at sea and his beloved ship. This man has been described as many things over the years, some good and some bad. He and I had had our fair share of squabbles but this time, he had earned his stripes. With Peter onboard, we gained renewed confidence; he'd know what to do.

CHAPTER 27

The Landward was back with us at precisely nine o'clock that morning, the crew repeating instructions for us to abandon our ship and go with them. This time, they kept adding that they could not be responsible for what might happen next, which was extremely unnerving to hear.

The DTI men unremittingly sailed around us, continuing to film the whole time. I had still not ventured outside and hoped to keep it that way as I did not want to be seen at any cost. I needed to keep my anonymity and to that end I stayed in the studio for the next couple of hours and continued with my programme, now networked on our Dutch station whilst we figured out the best course of action.

The sea was calm again that Saturday morning with hazy sunshine and a mist that prevented us seeing things too clearly if more than half a mile away. The Landward ceased its roaming and stationed itself fairly near the stern of the Ross Revenge; they had not tried to contact us for more than an hour. I wondered what was going on back in our London office, whereas on the radioship, we waited in anguish for the next development.

I considered it might be a repeat of Eurosiege, the surveillance exercise that had taken place a few years earlier. But unfortunately, this smelt unlike anything we had experienced before and I feared the worse. This was not going to end well, but still I could not fathom out what would happen. As long as Radio Caroline had been at sea in international waters, she had never been taken off the air by the authorities. So what was planned? What more could they do apart from keep up a blockade and prevent supplies reaching us? They could not hope to do that in the Landward, it was far too small; therefore there must be another plan.

The radio station crew wandered around in a trance. We all had the same feeling of helplessness, able to offer no insight into the situation if asked. Putting a positive spin on the whole affair seemed a pointless exercise as nobody felt anything but despair.

The DTI had been playing cat-and-mouse with us for more than twenty four hours and sooner or later something had to give; they held all the cards at the moment.

I continued to watch the Landward as again she started to circle round and round the Ross Revenge, and I suddenly remembered that I had seen this boat before; but just for a moment, I could not place it. Then, I remembered.

Weeks earlier, I had met Ronan and engineer Mike Watts, at Chatham railway station in Kent, and we had set off on an expedition to find tenders around the Medway ports. Driving down to Gillingham Pier, we had parked the car at the end of the slipway and walked back along the inlet. There were small children on the jetty casting lines into the river time and time again in pursuit of fish. Empty buckets of water lay at their feet; the fish were not biting that day.

Ronan and I reached the top of the inlet alongside the pier and we spotted a large blue and black launch, akin to a pilot cutter or police boat, moored alongside several warehouses.

'Hey, remember that boat, Nigel,' said Ronan. 'That would make it out to the Lady!'

I made a mental note to find out to whom it belonged and make some discreet enquiries next time I was on shore.

Now, out on the North Sea, I was looking at this boat again as it kept us under surveillance. I couldn't believe it; the DTI had actually chartered a boat in which Radio Caroline had been interested as a tender. But far worse, this boat was now part of some bigger plan to put the station off the air. These thoughts were spinning around in my head as I turned to look out from the port side of the bridge. Through the mist, off in the distance, I could make out the distinctive shape of an enormous bow wave; something large was moving pretty fast and heading across our stern, turning towards us as it drew level. I pressed the alarm button on the bridge and bells rang throughout the ship bringing people from all areas onto the deck. I ran into the studio to make sure something was still going out on the air to find Chris Kennedy, our Irish deejay, frantically searching for our theme tune, Caroline by the Fortunes, which we felt would need to be played at some point.

This new monstrosity on the sea, the tug *Volans*, was now coming up on the Ross Revenge from our stern and I could see uniformed men standing all the way down their port side as it came slowly up on our starboard quarter. As I arrived on deck, foam and spray belched up from side propellers, whilst they manoeuvred themselves alongside, and as soon as the two vessels touched, police and other agents from the boarding party made ready to jump across.

It was the first time I had been seen by the English DTI men, and as I ran along the deck, there were three men with stills cameras and a video camera all trained on me. They had numerous shots of all things by now and my arrival caused mild excitement as they reached down for their camera equipment, caught slightly off guard as other events were getting underway.

We were few in number but strong in spirit and stood along the deck as our home was raided and violated. The police were armed and would have used their weapons against us if they had felt it necessary. Contrary to some opinion in the media at the time, we had no weapons of any sort on board. Retaliation of that nature was not the way of Radio Caroline and we tried only to block the transference of this boarding party with our bodies.

One uniformed policeman did feel it necessary to remove his gun from its holster as he balanced between the two boats, smashing it into Peter Chicago's face in the process, causing a deep cut. Despite our resistance, within seconds our deck was swarming with the Dutch aggressors led by officers from the Dutch Radio Controle Dienst (RCD).

The DTI boat, meanwhile, watched from a short distance away as we were restrained and came under the rules of a foreign police force in international waters, where neither England nor Holland had any jurisdiction.

The whole affair so far had received a running commentary on the air, so nobody was in any doubt as to what had happened on this dreadful Saturday morning in nineteen eighty-nine.

It now became imperative for the illegal boarding party to get Caroline's transmitters off the air as soon as possible and the first thing for them to do was find the studios onboard.

By then, I had made it back to the studio and was in the process of telling others what had happened below when two policemen burst in and pulled us out of the room. Having been invited to comment on the air as to their actions, they said nothing and wrenched the cable from the microphone, thus silencing any further speech.

They forced the radio crew from the studio, pushing and shoving us in turn. This included deejay Caroline Martin who had a cassette snatched from her as she left; she was not allowed to keep it as it was evidence for possible prosecution. Caroline was on the ship with her boyfriend, Dave Asher and there was no preferential treatment as male and female were all pushed and manhandled in the same rough manner.

Meanwhile, Peter Chicago, face still bleeding, had been taken below and ordered to turn off all transmitters. Reluctantly, this is what he had to do, and whilst the equipment cooled down, the police made it their job to inspect every nook and cranny of the ship. We heard rumours that we were to be towed to Holland, where the ship would be impounded.

History was possibly about to repeat itself, for this is what happened in the sixties to the two Caroline ships only months after the passing of the Marine Offences Act.

This Act, brought into place to suppress the British offshore stations, could not prevent Radio Caroline staying on the air, except it had been creditors rather than any government that had caused Caroline to cease broadcasting. The two ships were boarded and eventually towed into Amsterdam.

It seemed to us now that the Ross Revenge was likely to suffer the same fate and be rendered unusable by a team of unwelcome visitors from Holland.

CHAPTER 28

The English and Dutch staff from Radio Caroline had been ordered to the messroom and thus had all movements restricted; accordingly, we waited for further information from our captors. Whilst the Dutch thugs concentrated on removing all equipment from our ship, the DTI men, whose boat had now tied up alongside the Volans, set about engaging in interviews with the English and Irish nationals onboard.

On this second trip to the Ross Revenge for the Landward, James Murphy, an investigator for the Office of Official Solicitor, acting on behalf of the Department of Trade and Industry, had come out to the ship and it was he who would conduct the intended interviews. We sat in the messroom, resigned to the situation, as Murphy came in and stood by the wall nearest the door. 'One by one, I want to talk to you. I'm sorry it has come to this, but things have got out of hand. Who's first?'

We were warned that refusal to follow instructions would mean arrest; it is clear now that these were no more than empty threats. But at the time, under such duress, we did not know what would happen.

I volunteered to go first, so that I could find out what was happening and maybe get an understanding of the situation. 'Where can we talk?' asked Murphy. 'Here,' I suggested, and led him into the small Overdrive studio at the back of the ship. It was a tight fit, for Murphy was not a small man and he now had a colleague in tow. This second man had been the main spokesman on the Landward over the last couple of days and was a tall, thin, sour looking man with a fixed expression; he held the same miserable grimace and slight snarled look the whole time. On the other hand, Murphy was straight out of *Oliver Twist*, a real Mr. Bumble. Red of face and round of stature, he seemed more out of place here than anybody and I'll wager he had really hoped we would leave the ship on demand, so these cosy little chats could be held in the security of his comfy office in London's Waterloo Bridge House.

He was ill-prepared and had many loose sheets of paper in a small briefcase into which he plunged his chubby hands on several occasions. 'Okay', he said breathlessly. 'What's your name?'

Should I conform or stick up for my rights as a free British citizen in international waters? These rights, so important to the British Government when they require them to be, were waived on this Saturday morning.

'You have no rights out here', I replied cautiously, continuing, 'So that's it then?' I did not feel brave, I was resigned to my fate, whatever it may be; I knew, of course, that would not be the end of it.

The reply was instant, almost rehearsed. 'Unless you answer my questions, you will be arrested and taken to a police station ashore where your identity will be established.' This of course was nonsense, but as they had gone this far, nothing was beyond the realms of possibility.

I told him I was called John Thomas; my father's Christian name and my mother's maiden name. I did not mean it to come out in quite that manner, but that's the way it did, and Murphy said nothing. I realised my accidental innuendo immediately. I was asked how I got my job on Caroline, who was my first boss, where the tenders were based and even Ronan's current involvement. All basic stuff requiring little thought on my part to fabricate information.

All Murphy required, I imagined, were some names and a few facts on his sheet of paper and he would be happy. He knew the answers I gave that afternoon were all nonsense, but he had some of his questions answered and that seemed good enough for him; I knew the others in our party would be similarly evasive. To round off my afternoon session with Jim Murphy, I was told my actions would be reported to the Director of Public Prosecutions for possible further action.

While the questioning continued with other members of Caroline's team, the stripping of the ship's equipment started in earnest with the total removal of anything ever used in the transmission of a Dutch language station on the Ross Revenge. We were told that as Radio Caroline's English studio had been used from time to time for Dutch transmissions, this too, would be removed. They appeared to have a lot of knowledge about our operations onboard, some due no doubt, to infiltration of the company.

This was pretty easy, as access to the ship on anorak visits was quite normal on the Ross Revenge. Visiting boats would arrive alongside, possibly with DTI men hidden amongst the fans. A guided tour of the ship was always guaranteed and the men from the ministry could then go home, rewarded.

In the days of the Mi Amigo, we had been very careful as to who was allowed on the ship. Visitors were not permitted onboard for it was the only way to keep the authorities off the boat. Things had become woefully relaxed on that front with the Ross Revenge.

The deck of the Volans was filling up with Caroline's broadcasting equipment, from transmitter parts to records, CDs, carts, clocks, and even studio chairs.

The raiders had planned to cut down both fore and aft radio towers, which included our recently completed front mast, but when told they could actually fall on their ship, they changed their minds and decided instead to cut down the aerial array which hung between the two masts.

Our new insulator on deck was smashed up too. This had only been recently installed after the previous one was destroyed during the collapse of our three hundred foot tower.

It had been hard work and a mission of extreme danger in ferrying this weighty insulator out to sea and lifting it aboard. To see it hauled away and smashed was even more heartbreak for us to watch. The Dutch boarding party were hooligans, with precious few rules save for destroying Radio Caroline.

Later in the afternoon, the press arrived in the form of television helicopters; one flying low enough for us to see the ITN logo on its underside.

Calls were made to the coastguard by the Ross Revenge as the raiders came aboard. We were in a state of distress and were being swarmed over by armed police in international waters. When we called for assistance, we were brushed off with a prepared statement: 'This is a government sponsored action and as such, we cannot comment.'

It was the most unbelievable of statements by an organisation in place to save and protect lives at sea that I had ever heard. If something had gone wrong during this raid, it would probably have been the subject of an almighty cover-up. Governments are not immune from killing and injuring people as they carry out their actions.

All subsequent calls made from our ship went unanswered. Not much of a coastguard service, I thought at the time.

The destruction continued and piece-by-piece our beloved radio station was taken apart by this criminal contingent, answerable to no-one.

We were now allowed to move about the ship on the upper decks and visit our cabins, whilst the engine room and transmitter room remained out of bounds. It was not easy having these restrictions in place, when only a few hours before, we were free to roam around what was our home.

CHAPTER 29

Around five in the afternoon, the deck of the Volans was strewn with our equipment. Everything that could have some connection with broadcasting seemed to lie either on the deck or be crated up under tarpaulins. Our mixers lay surrounded by thousands of records, with cart machines buried under long stretches of copper wiring; electrical cables curled around the ever growing mass. A substantial part of Radio Caroline's history had been unceremoniously dumped on the deck of a tug.

A strange, but welcome, decision was made in the late afternoon as a call went out to everyone involved in the raid to assemble on the Volans for dinner. One by one, the raiders left our ship, together with the men from the DTI. We had the ship to ourselves and set about seeing if anything remained that could be of use in the future. Peter headed for the transmitter room and was amazed to find several important parts still sitting on the floor, ready for removal. These were immediately hidden and the search continued for any more parts that could be useful if we managed to get back on the air.

I was out on the back deck in the fading sunshine. The weather was warm and the day had been long with our unwelcome visitors into their sixth hour on board. A lot of people stood about, their work done, waiting for instructions as to their next move. The arc lights from the Ross Revenge shone ahead and out to sea, whilst those from the Volans bathed our deck in a bright but orange-tinged glow. Making my way up to our bridge, I spotted Martin Roumen, leader of the boarding party from the Dutch PTT; I took the plunge and went to talk to him. He had been refusing to discuss anything with the English crew onboard all day, and I grabbed the opportunity to find out what lay behind the day's events.

'Have you finished your job yet?' I enquired. 'There's not much left to do now', he replied, leaning forward on the railings as he looked down onto the deck of the Volans. 'But one thing is sure and I know this to be true; Caroline will come back on the air. We are leaving your ship here and you will get started again, but,' and he turned to face me, 'make sure you have no Dutch programmes on the air and no Dutch commercials and you will not see us again. Keep it that way and we will stay away from you. It's up to you now, so be careful.'

I did not get a chance to reply; he was called away by one of his team from the Volans, and he left me with my thoughts.

The original plan was to tow the ship away, but this had been cancelled in the late afternoon from a higher authority. The authorities decided it would cause too much adverse publicity having the radioship in a Dutch harbour, as it could become a focal point for the press and Radio Caroline fans. They knew the raid was totally illegal, and a court case would no doubt demand they hand the ship back to Caroline.

No mention of our shortwave transmissions was made on that day and during my brief conversation with the Martin Roumen, the subject did not arise. But evidently, Roumen was not going to discuss tactics with me.

However, months earlier, the DTI had been contacted by the FBI regarding Radio New York International, a short-lived American offshore station, whose owners were now behind Caroline's new shortwave religious service, World Mission Radio.

The U.S. station had used Radio Caroline's continued existence in their defence when arguing why their radioship should not have been raided by the FBI in international waters. The British and American governments then had discussions regarding the offshore radio situation in Europe and Radio Caroline's continued existence on the North Sea; this caused acute embarrassment in Whitehall. The Dutch authorities were called in and discussions took place on how to end this so-called offshore spectacle.

The shortwave transmissions from the Ross Revenge were on 6.215 kHz, and the channel was internationally registered as a marine emergency frequency. It still is, although even in the twenty first century, some licensed stations have broadcast on or close to that frequency with impunity, RTE in Ireland being one of many. (Source: WRN via DX Listening Digest)

There was a tentative Dutch connection to the World Mission Radio programmes in Holland, and the government in that country were more than willing to use this slight detail to help the British in their quest to silence the Ross Revenge. It was never on the cards for these two European governments to let Caroline continue; both Britain and Holland were determined to kill off Radio Caroline once and for all.

The Dutch have never been shy when it comes to raiding offshore broadcasters and they agreed to front a raid on the Ross Revenge. They had asked the Thatcher government years earlier for permission to mount a raid, when they felt threatened by Radio Monique, but this had been turned down. It was not until the arrival of Laser and the threat of more ships that the English began to think of stronger lines of action; thus, the die was cast.

All throughout the day, the English DTI men were at pains to state that this raid was a purely Dutch endeavour, and they were there only as observers, no more. This may have been the case on the day, whilst they allowed the Dutch to carry out the dirty work, but the English certainly had soiled hands when it came to concocting the attack.

James Murphy still had not questioned Peter Chicago and intercepted him on the deck. 'Please, I want to talk to you!' he pleaded again and again.

Peter walked away saying nothing, much to the annoyance of the portly DTI man, who now had to continue after him at a fairly fast pace. The poor man looked exhausted after the day's escapades and slouched forward before picking up speed, gripping his sheaf of papers as he went. After a day such as this, he must have longed for his desk in London. He lost Peter on the first turn.

We had not seen a single boat anywhere near our ship all day except the Olau ferry, this time sailing even further away than ever before, which we thought unusual. We later found out there had been an exclusion zone set up around our ship, so nobody was allowed anywhere near the Ross Revenge.

Unexpectedly, a small boat was spotted heading our way from the Kent coast but was still about half an hour away. The DTI men started to hurry things along, gathering up all their bits and pieces and making final attempts to collar Peter Chicago. Meanwhile, the Volans began making ready to leave as our visitors arrived on the scene. Martin Roumen ran down to the deck and jumped across to his ship as engines revved and ropes were being untied. I watched from the bridge and heard our ship's radio crackle into life as I heard someone on the bridge of the Volans call the Landward. 'What a great day. We all deserve medals!' 'Too right,' came the reply, as the Volans turned to face out to sea and set off for Holland with all our precious equipment and our Dutch radio colleagues. They had been arrested and were going ashore to face the consequences. I watched the Volans pull away, with a feeling of hatred for these government men coursing through my veins.

Our new arrival turned out to be our official tender with Dave the Fish, members of the press and several people from the London office. It was such a relief to see friends and I ran down to the lower deck as they arrived alongside.

The man on the bows of the Fairwind was an Australian called

Warwick Armstrong who was based in London for most of the time but who had spent some weeks on the Ross Revenge as chief engineer. 'Permission to come aboard, Captain!' he bellowed several times over the roaring engines. All attempts to interrogate Chicago had now ceased and the DTI men clambered back onboard their vessel. The Landward untied and moved to the other side of our ship to get a better look at the visitors. They must have been incensed to have had their operation surveyed in such close detail by members of our land team.

The DTI men took pictures of the Fairwind and those standing around her deck, then the Landward turned for England, the whole ensemble having been involved in a day of unrivalled butchery and illegality. Meanwhile, our new arrivals took stock of the situation.

It was time to inspect the damage, now unhindered by the thugs who were onboard all day. We had the shock of lives when we saw the state of the studios and record library. They had been ripped to shreds and every piece of equipment, record and tape had been removed. It was the same story in the transmitter room with every valve removed or broken and every wire cut to pieces.

The damage was far worse than I could ever have imagined. Even the fuel-injection pump on the second generator had been attacked with a hammer, leaving us with just one engine; a new pump would cost the organisation a staggering one thousand pounds. If we now lost our only working generator for any reason, we would be without power, so this wanton vandalism could have put us in a great deal of peril out on the high seas, especially at night. I went to bed in a state of shock and disbelief, sleeping fitfully for an hour or so before wandering upstairs and watching television in the messroom on my own.

What on earth were we to do? The ship was still ours and I was sure we could get some sort of signal on the air again, but I knew how low our finances were, and with absolutely no income, survival would be difficult, if not impossible. The main problem for now was supplying the radioship; the DTI had broken our organisation wide open and knew everything about all our land support team and tenders. They had already warned boat owners of dire consequences if any association with Radio Caroline was continued. We were at our lowest ebb.

CHAPTER 30

In the days after the raid, we started to rebuild the ship and Peter decided it would be a good idea if we could get the towers completed and a new aerial strung up between them. This was a lot easier said than done, and our intrepid team spent many long dangerous hours heaving new sections up to the top of the mast . Pulling these heavy sections up and placing one on top of another, nearly one hundred feet above a moving deck, was bordering on madness, and willingness to partake in this episode was tantamount to suicide.

Chicago stayed on deck level to oversee the events taking place high in the sky and took on the task of principle winch man; a brave few continued to climb day after day to complete the task. It was sheer back breaking work and after the top section of the rear tower crashed to the deck whilst the riggers were in the mast, it was decided that the height would be reduced by twenty feet. As the highest part of the mast came crashing down, I was filming the proceedings from the top of the funnel. We all froze where we were, as we had no idea where the heavy section would land. Thankfully, no injuries were received by anyone.

Later on, in the course of attaching the aerial wires to the top of the back mast in the dead of night, a very brave Dave Asher froze to the spot in sheer panic. I climbed a fair way up to try and talk to him but this was a particular nightmare for me due to my severe fear of heights. Dave did manage to climb down though, having accomplished his amazingly difficult task. Fortunately, the array had already been attached to the front mast by a professional rigger whilst we built the back tower.

Another colleague climbed the back tower late one night and threatened to throw himself off, blaming to the trauma he suffered throughout the raid. He was talked down and fortunately did not carry out his promised threat.

We all had our own ways of dealing with the situation in which we found ourselves, and the hard work did help, leaving us all so tired there was little time for fretting.

Peter Chicago spent many long hours rebuilding one of the smaller transmitters, using bits and pieces rescued on the day of the raid. More spares came out from land including a studio mixer and various other forms of equipment needed to resume broadcasting. Even my mother handed over several hundred pounds towards the new main output valve.

A rally was held in London several weeks after the raid with many hundreds of people marching in support of Radio Caroline. Supplies were donated and collected, ready to be taken to the ship. We had remained off the air for the duration of the repair work and hoped to get fuel and food out to the ship before turning on the transmitters. Doing it this way, we hoped, would enable us to stock up the Ross Revenge with essentials before a probable watch on the ship resumed. However, there were some in the organisation who thought differently, and broadcasting resumed before we could get our supply boat out to the Ross Revenge. The skipper of the tender then refused to do the run as it was deemed too risky; thus a search for another tender got underway, delaying our deliveries by several weeks.

Back on the air now on our former frequency of five-five-eight kilohertz medium wave, a skeleton service got underway. But the British government still had more tricks up their sleeves. They allocated the frequency to a new London station called Spectrum Radio, effectively jamming our signal. Even the *Daily Telegraph* media section became involved and advised us to change frequencies.

It was making us out to be the rebels, because we were seen by the general public as broadcasting on a frequency used by a legitimate station and the publicity was not good. We had to move channels but some of our group were keen to fight it out in the hope we could win. I had other ideas and fought my corner long and hard when in London with Peter Moore and finally we moved to eight-one-nine kilohertz after Peter's long hours of argument with Chicago.

The only real money to be had now was from Solar Video, the merchandise business I had set up a few months earlier. We printed more t-shirts, designed new stickers and put lots of adverts on the air hoping our listeners would buy everything we had in stock, and then want more. As soon as the money arrived, it was spent immediately on supplying the Ross Revenge.

I came off the ship after a few weeks in a large sea going rubberboat driven by the ever vigilant Warwick, who spent more time trying to restart the outboard motor than actually driving the boat. Our return trip even included a close pass from a police boat, while also visible was a low-flying plane, taking more than a healthy interest in us. We eventually limped into a harbour near Rochester in Kent, having run out of petrol, just short of our destination. We received a tow from a small yacht returning from France and headed for Peter Moore's boat, moored in Hoo

Marina. This boat was undergoing reconstruction, and as such, Peter spent many weekends onboard, slowing building, cutting and grinding with some success; we were to stay the night on this boat and head home in the morning.

Emotions ran high that night and Dave Richards, who had come off the ship with presenter Neil Gates and me, decided to resurrect the programme controller argument, this time fueled with drink. I had remained sober that night, and when threatened with more verbal abuse and a wallop from Richards as he lunged at me, I decided that escape was the best form of defence and so shot out of my chair onto the deck.

Unfortunately for my assailant, he took a short cut to catch me and slipped over in a pile of sick deposited by the other drunken returnee, Gates, minutes before. It was not a pretty sight to see him thrash around in the vomit, but my goodness, it was very funny. He did not catch me that night and when sober in the morning, he remembered little of the incident. However, in later years, egged on by his girlfriend, he decided I was a particularly unsavoury character and ended all contact with me.

Luck was on Radio Caroline's side surprisingly, as we found twenty tons of fuel onboard which had been secretly siphoned off and hidden in spare tanks over the previous years as a back-up supply. Engineers had continually hidden the odd ton here and there for emergencies and it had been forgotten about, until now; I had no idea it was there.

But diesel is used up at a phenomenal rate on powerful generators such as those onboard the Ross Revenge and even though we ran on low power and curtailed our hours, the fuel was quickly running out. The bills mounted fast, the generators requiring at least four tons a week for the ship to operate.

The English organisation was on its own and we had to feed the staff on the ship, pay for tenders and now the fuel, formerly supplied by the Dutch operation. Large amounts of fresh water had to be delivered at the same time and no supply run was complete without cigarettes and alcohol, both expensive items that really bit into the limited budget.

I ordered the fuel from Jentex in Ramsgate and a tanker met us by the jetty in Herne Bay. Dave the Fish was now our only tender and his boat, the Fairwind, was not large, so the best we could do was place three or four large barrels on his deck and pump them full of fuel. Bemused looks from the tanker driver were the least of our worries as we scoured the streets for any suspicious looking vehicles with prying DTI men and secretive policemen, who would be eager and more than happy to arrest us.

I sat at the roadside and paid for the fuel in cash; fifty pounds notes as a rule, and lots of them. Another wad of cash went to Dave and even more was spent in the supermarket on a shopping run.

We eventually got a fairly reliable service on the air thanks to Peter Chicago's hard work in the transmitter room. But Radio Caroline was suffering from increased DTI activity, making the day-to-day running so very gruelling. It was not long before we lost Solar Video as the DTI closed down the box number in London and paid me a visit at home with the usual warnings of prosecution over the selling of merchandise. While they were at it, another warning not to go back to the ship was forthcoming from a peeved James Murphy. I had already been warned of the illegality of my actions when officials spoke to me during the raid. So, unsurprisingly, two days after their home visit, I was back at sea with the Ross Revenge, gradually watching as conditions worsened; by degrees, everything began to run out. Supplies donated after the raid had dwindled to next-to-nothing and we were now going off the air even earlier each night.

But that turned out to be the least of our problems though, as an almighty storm hit us in January, nineteen-ninety which put us off the air and even caused the DTI men in London to be concerned for us. I answered the phone on the bridge at the height of the storm to find it was Jim Murphy from the DTI, concerned for our welfare. I told him we were all okay, and we would be back on the air as soon as the storm abated; he wished us good luck and hung up.

Meanwhile, the ship was buried in huge walls of water as she took a battering from stem to stern, the like of which I had not experienced in years; it was more severe than the storm that brought our mast down and this current anchorage provided no protection from sandbanks. The close proximity of sandbanks could quell some of the ferocity of the waves, but here in the Fall's Head, there were none. Our previous anchorage in the Knock Deep did offer some protection.

We sat on top of mountainous crests looking into what seemed like bottomless pits of water as we began our plunge into the swirling cauldron; it was frightening and I thought at times we would not come through it. I had been through many severe storms during my time with Radio Caroline, and each new one seemed to surpass the others.

One crewmember was so scared, he curled up in a ball on the floor in the newsroom behind the bridge, shivering and whimpering. He had a look of sheer terror etched across his face, his eyes wide and staring. I gripped the railings nearby and peered out through the windows down across the bows and into the storm.

It was then that I got the shock of my life as I saw a man on the front deck in all weather gear climbing into the forepeak hold. 'Who the hell is that?' I screamed. 'What idiot is out there?'

Getting out onto the deck in this weather was impossible, as I discovered on trying to open the doorway to have a look for this stupid man; the winds were just too severe. Deciding against the idea, I did a head count inside the ship and found everybody to be accounted for, either in their cabins or on the bridge. So who was it? The sight of this sailor was real and vivid; I had no reason to doubt his presence.

Now, years later, I have discovered the strange story concerning the Ross Revenge ghost, a friendly one by all accounts, who had the ship's safety in mind at all times.

The tale tells of a fisherman who fell into the sea years earlier from the Ross Revenge when she was fishing in the Arctic Circle. He was never seen again. But had I seen him on that stormy afternoon? I believe I did, but at the time, it just added to my state of confusion as we battled the waves.

The storm eased a little into the night and it looked as if we had come through reasonably unscathed. As with all bouts of bad weather, the major concern is for the anchor to hold, and on this occasion, it did not let us down.

Remembering the observations of Captain Ernie on the night we lost the three hundred foot mast, gave me some comfort. He had nonchalantly mentioned that the ship could go right over but would right itself again, although we should hold on tightly during the ride. I'm not sure I believed him, but it helped calm my nerves.

As the weeks wore on, the living conditions onboard became increasingly grim and the atmosphere was becoming very difficult; several of the crew were not even on speaking terms and it became clear that two very different camps were forming. Some went out of their way to be insufferable and at one point, I became particularly unwell, and unaware of what was happening on the air. Unable to even get out of bed, I heard reports of anarchy taking place in the studios. I had made up my mind to turn the transmitters off if this nonsense continued but I naturally hoped it would all calm down.

Several deejays, including our capricious Geordie, Neil Gates, went on strike over conditions as we struggled to survive, and he presented music only shows, speaking occasionally to describe conditions on the ship. Neil resigned whilst still onboard with an unfortunate announcement.

It was Friday, the sixteenth of February, nineteen-ninety and I had been very ill for over a week, still unable to get out of bed. Gates finished his final programme with this statement: *'Five minutes to nine o'clock from Caroline. This is the last time you will be hearing me, Neil Gates, on Caroline. This decision has been forced upon me by the management's couldn't-care-less attitude displayed to the crew of the Ross Revenge. Caroline is supposed to be a hit music radio station, yet we have not received any new records for more than two months. This failing by the management does not stop at records but extends to all the basic necessities that we require for our day-to-day existence here on the Ross Revenge. This is the last record from me. Enjoy listening to Caroline; it probably won't be here much longer. Bye from me.'*

Neil wrote down an abbreviated version of this resignation speech, and handed it to me.

As he was reading his statement on the air, a tender was already making its way to the ship with supplies and a replacement crew.

At the time, I was disappointed and angry with Neil. But on reflection, times were extremely difficult, tempers frayed and with the possibility of another raid likely at anytime, it made people think and react in ways they may not have done otherwise.

I could not influence Neil's feelings for the Caroline management or magically improve the conditions onboard but I wished his behaviour towards me at the time could have contained a little less vitriol.

Another presenter, who remained on the ship after I had left for shore leave, did not take kindly to Neil's earlier outburst and announced his home address on the air, which under the circumstances could only have acerbated the situation. It did make me smile at the time, but by then I needed a laugh.

This was not the end of the silliness though, as one of our visiting deejays, a man called Chris Cooper who came out to the ship for one trip only, did not approve of the music policy of the time. He went home and wrote a reproachful piece for the publication, Horizon magazine, condemning the music format we ran and the behaviour of some of those onboard. It was then sold to listeners through one of the Caroline fan clubs. The whole system was falling apart and nobody seemed able stop it.

Every Tom, Dick and Harry with little or no broadcasting experience seemed to know better. All and sundry thought they could play and say what they wanted on the air. I fought long and hard against this anarchy, judiciously in my opinion, but it caused me even more problems onboard as the incumbents continued to argue.

Sadly, the troublemakers won the day and it became more or less impossible to manage the station. Caroline had a broadcast team, the majority of whom had never been in a radio studio before, whose propriety on the air was poor, to say the least.

Peter Moore miraculously managed to find a modest amount of money after much trial and tribulation and Dave the Fish came out with the tender a few more times, taking me back to the Ross Revenge after some shore leave. We were still playing cat and mouse with the DTI, but even Dave had to relent in the end after pressure from the authorities became too severe.

He was taken to London, questioned, shown a whole series of photographs and asked to identify people as required. Pictures showed me on the jetty in Herne Bay paying for the diesel; our surveillance of the streets, watching out for DTI spies, had not paid off particularly well. Dave denied knowing anyone.

The adventure at sea was not to last, and at the end of November, nineteen ninety, the station closed down for the night and never came back on the air; generator problems and lack of fuel due to the company's financial position, had silenced the radio station.

We needed time to regroup and get things back on a sensible level and to that end, we had numerous meetings in London. However, any plans we made would be deemed immediately redundant, for going through parliament at the time was the new Broadcast Bill, which effectively ended Radio Caroline. It gave the armed forces permission to board any unlicenced radio station on the high seas, wherever it was situated, if the signal could be received in Britain. It was an unbelievably draconian piece of legislation but the Conservative government of the day had done some pretty diabolical things already in their attempts to silence Caroline.

Marine lawyers said at the time in television interviews that a ship laden with crack cocaine could sail with impunity through the high seas untouched, but Radio Caroline could be boarded by the armed forces and her crew arrested.

When the bill became law at the start of nineteen-ninety one, the DTI took extra interest in the Ross Revenge and even though off the air, we had to get permission to run supplies out to the people on the ship and on several occasions they simply refused to allow us to use any tenders. Our resources were low and the adverse publicity had scared off all boat owners, apart from Dave the Fish. Nonetheless, the DTI continued to make supplying the ship as difficult as they possibly could and Dave was advised to question this in writing. He wrote to James Murphy at the Department of Trade and Industry, thus:

'Dear Mr. Murphy, Following our recent discussions concerning the propriety of my supplying essentials to the crew onboard the "Ross Revenge", I have taken legal advice in light of the threats you have made against me personally and my property. I am advised that, as Radio Caroline has not been broadcasting in contravention of recently introduced legislation and as (I am informed by the operators and crew of the "Ross Revenge") no transmissions will be made in breach of current legislation, there is no basis whatsoever upon which you can seek to challenge the entitlement of those onboard the "Ross Revenge" to receive necessary supplies, nor my entitlement to provide or transport them, should I feel so inclined. Should you continue with your threatening behaviour, I will have no option but to refer this matter to my solicitors. Should you be so foolish as to carry out your threats, I will sue both you and those by whom you are employed for damages for tortious interference in my legitimate business.'

One of our Dutch colleagues, however, thought that Easter, ninety ninety-one was a perfect time for Caroline to make a reappearance, and at Peter Moore's behest, I recorded a special programme on tape to be broadcast on shortwave. This was done using equipment belonging to a fellow chorister from my church and sent across to Holland. Both the DTI and the Dutch PTT were running around in circles trying to trace the transmissions, as they appeared at first glance, to be coming from the North Sea. It was not a big deal, but it shows how desperate the authorities were in their endeavours to remove all traces of Radio Caroline from the airwaves. The transmissions actually came from Amsterdam and we smiled at the consequences of that Easter Day.

Meanwhile, the Ross Revenge remained at sea, off the air, and under continued DTI surveillance, with a skeleton crew onboard. Ronan O' Rahilly continued to scour the globe for a country willing to supply Caroline with a license to broadcast; none was ever forthcoming.

CHAPTER 31

As nineteen ninety-one continued, our ship sat silently on the North Sea and it was looking more and more likely that Caroline would never broadcast again. Spring was giving way to summer and tenders were still running out to the ship with occasional DTI permission. My major concern was where my future lay and much thought went into that endeavour.

I drove into Whitstable harbour in Kent in early May with the car laden down with supplies for the ship. I had been to London to see my long suffering friend Peter Moore very early that morning, only to be greeted with news that more deals had fallen through and there was still no licence available to us; the news came as no surprise as we were just grabbing at straws. I set off for the coast.

I did not know it at the time, but that was to be the end of my association with Radio Caroline while she remained at sea. I had applied for work abroad and later that same day, my mother drove me to Gatwick airport where I flew off to Tel Aviv for yet another pirate adventure; this time it was the Voice of Peace.

So many friends had already been to the VOP and I was doing it much later than most, but at least it would be good to see what it was really like after hearing so many stories over the years. A nice break away from England too, after the dreadful experiences of the past few months.

Flying low over the sea on approaching the airport, I saw two radioships several miles off the coast of Tel Aviv and felt more excited than I had in a long time.

The first thing to hit me was the intense heat. Walking off the plane into the fresh air at Ben Gurion Airport had been like walking into a furnace and I stood still for a moment shutting my eyes, allowing the warmth to soak into me.

I headed into the complex and through customs towards the bus terminal, hoping there might be someone from the radio station to meet me; there was nobody, naturally.

The bus ride through unknown territory left me dazed as our mad Israeli driver seemed to have a death wish; it felt as if we took corners at forty-five degrees times. Driving etiquette in the Middle East was a tad less dignified than in England and horns blazed and fists shook at every opportunity whilst we pushed onwards into the city centre. I had told the driver where I needed to be dropped off and hoped he would remember.

Alighting from the bus on a corner after we came to a sudden stop, I was told by the driver, 'It is over there!' I grabbed my suitcases and with some relief, stepped down from the bus as it screeched off into the night, horn blazing away yet again.

The Hotel Astor, near the sea-front, was a three star hotel and the VOP had an arrangement whereby those on shore leave could have use of a room with two beds. I headed for the room on the third floor and threw my bags down with a great deal of relief. It was not a luxurious room by any stretch of the imagination, but it was adequate. There were two beds at right angles to each other and a very odd looking red television in one corner. But now, I needed food and so headed across the busy road to a small restaurant for dinner and some much needed alcohol.

I was to have some company later on from a VOP deejay who was on shore leave and due to come with me to the ship the next day. His name was Alex Rogers and I already knew him from the final dark days of Radio Caroline.

Next morning, the call came from the office and we were to meet the VOP car outside the hotel and head off to the harbour. But first we must get to the supermarket and buy vodka, as there was a no alcohol rule on the ship. I could not believe this news, but I was glad we had an opportunity to buy some liquor before setting off to sea.

On arrival at the harbour, the police took my passport which was the done thing with all the crew heading for the VOP. I was told it would be returned when I left the country and so we headed off towards the radioship, anchored a few miles off the coast.

The water I had been used to in the North Sea became a distant memory as we chugged across the deep blue Mediterranean and got ever nearer the Peaceship.

She had been broadcasting since the early seventies and in her former years had sailed up and down the coast, broadcasting messages of peace and love to the fighting Arabs and Israelis. I was there twenty-one years later and things had only just settled down after the first Gulf War. Scud missiles from Iraq had flown out over the Mediterranean beyond the Peaceship having missed their Jewish targets. Presenters and crew onboard at the time were issued with special masks by the Israeli authorities in case of a gas attack, but luckily there was never a need to use them.

The Peaceship had been anchored off Tel Aviv for many years by now, and had become much more of a commercial venture by the nineteen nineties.

The manager of the station was a man called Reuven who ran the day to day goings on, sought out any advertisers and organised the tenders. He was a pleasant enough fellow whose actions seemed more school masterly than manager.

The big boss, Abie Nathan, the man who ran the whole business, was originally from Persia and had lived in Bombay while growing up. He was now a sixty-three year old, who years earlier had flown with the RAF.

More recently, he had attempted on numerous occasions to instigate peace missions with Egypt, and also tried to get a law overturned that forbade contact with the Palestine Liberation Organisation and other paramilitary groups; he met Yasser Arafat for peace talks several times and endured prison sentences as a result.

During my time in Israel, Abie was a free man but on hunger strike. This was due to his treatment by the authorities, resulting from his most recent visit to Palestine. He was in an hotel room taking only water and the occasional biscuit, but getting massive amounts of publicity in the press and on television and radio. Meanwhile, I was on the way out to his radio station on the calm blue Mediterranean in the glorious sunshine. How different this was to the North Sea and how I wished Caroline could be here instead of in Europe, suffering at the hands of the brutish DTI.

The journey took less than half an hour, and soon we were alongside the Peaceship, watching our baggage being ferried aboard. I was first up the ladder and onto the deck, glancing all around as I stepped down from the railings which ran along the side of the ship.

There was that wonderful smell of diesel again wafting through my nostrils, but this time the generators were above deck, towards the stern of the ship, pumping power into the vessel on this hot summer's day.

It was almost noon and I looked along the deck for someone who might be taking an interest in me; there is nothing worse than being a new arrival in such a situation. I felt awkward and looked around for company and instructions. My travelling companion, Alex, had already disappeared inside the ship, no doubt already bored with my company. Eventually, presenter John McDonald came to my aid and welcoming me aboard, took me to my new cabin.

It was a reasonable sized room with twin bunks. However, there were not enough people on the ship for anyone to share, so that afforded some privacy. The m.v. Peace was staffed by a captain, several Filipino crew and an Indian cook called Radha, who was the friendliest of them all and fortunately, an Anglophile.

The ship was freshly painted and well ordered. Ropes were neatly laid out on the front deck ready for use next time the ship was in port. She was higher out of the water than either the Ross Revenge or the Mi Amigo and had a tendency to roll considerably on the swell.

Meals were at set times and greatly looked forward to as Radha was a first class cook, and I thought how popular he would have been on the North Sea.

Tendering the ship for water and fuel in the Mediterranean was easily accomplished; we simply sailed into port, Ashdod in the main, which was about thirty or so miles south of Tel Aviv. We bunkered up and set sail again, the only stipulation being that the station turn off its transmitters whilst in port, as the men who worked on the cranes would get an electrical shock as the signal from the ship went into the metalwork and then into them.

The m.v. Peace was a veteran ship, already about sixty years old when I arrived, but as with the other radioships I had worked on, this one gave me no real cause for concern. After all it was the height of summer and the sea was incredibly flat at times; only the occasional swell caused things to become a little uncomfortable.

The sight of land just a few miles away was a little unnerving after Caroline's existence so many miles out to sea but it wasn't long before I got used to it. Through the binoculars from the bridge, the beach looked enticing and busy but it would be two weeks before I was to go ashore again. Out on the ship, the weather remained beautiful and the people were friendly.

A couple of deejays had been working for the VOP for several years now, namely John McDonald and former Caroline presenter, Kenny Page; they had become key players on the station. Other visiting deejays would usually stay for the six month contract, as I would, and leave for a local radio job in England, if they could find one. My other colleagues around this time were Rob Haywood, Mark Taylor, Alex Skinner and Dominic Hill.

We usually did two shows a day, broken by a little sunbathing and watching television on the rather limited service from Israel; Channel One or Two were the only options. Not much else reached the ship out in the Mediterranean except a very poor quality signal from Jordan. Luckily,

Israeli television showed a lot of English and American shows with Hebrew subtitles, so we could cope under the circumstances. Dinner time was usually accompanied by old episodes of Hart to Hart or Columbo and a bit later, the daily offering was Saved by the Bell, a real favourite of mine.

Meals were pretty good on the whole with plenty of fresh fruit and vegetables. We had a supply boat at least twice a week and this was eagerly anticipated as it brought our mail from home as well as our food and supplies.

At mealtimes, the deejays sat at one end of a small two-sided table. Mouth watering smells from the galley caused the always hungry deejays to occasionally bang on the table demanding service, much to the amusement of a smiling Radha. There was a small television at the end of the galley on a shelf which meant a bit of craning round to see, but it was contact with the outside world, which was always a bonus.

The ship's crew ate separately and contact with them was paltry to say the least. I can't remember too many conversations with any of them apart from the captain who would bring the weather forecast into the studio each afternoon around five-thirty; even then it was only pleasantries with a man whose English was pretty limited.

Some members of the crew would spend a whole year at sea before going ashore and then go on home to the Philippines with their salary which was a fortune in their country.

However, as is probably quite normal under the circumstances, some crew went a little stir crazy in the confined and rather cramped conditions aboard the Peaceship. Some would walk around the ship, gazing out towards the shore and saying nothing whilst giving the English disdaining looks; such was the relationship with these fellows at times. The captain was the laziest man I had ever met and even I could have done his job with my eyes closed. He never ventured from his cabin until after lunch and proceeded to strut about like a prison guard.

We had a nasty problem with cockroaches on the ship, something I found somewhat disconcerting when I first came across these creatures, but I got used to them, and after a while they became no more than a mere nuisance.

These horrible creatures seemed to live mainly in the smaller messroom and galley areas where it was warmer and food scraps could be easily found. They hid in the nooks and crannies during daylight hours waiting for darkness to descend and the ship's daily business to cease, before coming out to feast.

It was the done thing when entering the galley to bang a mug down or slap your hand on the counter. This sent the little blighters scurrying off to their various hideouts and a quick wipe with a disinfectant soaked cloth gave some peace of mind in the preparation of any midnight snack.

This exercise was all well and good in the main. But one particularly quiet night with little to do, I decided to make a mug of tea to take to the cabin where I was to begin my charge of writing letters home. The ship's crew were, as usual, watching the small television in the galley. It was always an amusing sight as they struggled to understand the English language and Hebrew subtitles in some old Columbo murder-mystery movie and they argued amongst themselves as to the twists and turns of the plot.

As I walked towards the water heater, I could see that the cockroaches had popped out for their midnight feast and were scurrying around on the surface adjacent to the water nozzle.

It seemed the crew did not see me enter from the far end of the galley and were nattering away as I slammed a plate down with great force into the midst of the nightly visitors. They were gone in an instant, apart from the ones who took the force of my weapon.

My pleasure at removing these horrible creatures was short lived as almost at once I heard a blood-curdling scream, and on looking across the room, saw one of the ship's Filipino crewmembers grab a long knife from under the table and leap in my direction.

He gave a terrifyingly loud shriek, equivalent to a war cry, and in a bound was across the table and behind me. It all happened so quickly, for I had only a moment to glance round and throw myself through the doorway and out onto the deck. Ringing in my ears were the man's screams, 'I kill you, English! I kill you, English!' He managed to get hold of my t-shirt as I struggled to keep my balance and I turned to grab his wrist and hold it back to afford protection from the knife but he was too strong and angry and I was losing the battle.

On reaching the deck, the t-shirt tore from my body as I fell onto the stairway which led to a long corridor with the studios and cabins. I tried to scramble into the ship and escape below, but kept losing my footing; I was fully expecting this madman to slice through the back of my head. Mostly on my backside, I slid down the metal stairs, cutting my back several times and finally made it to my cabin. On slamming the door shut, I stood against the opposite wall, desperate for breath, my heart pounding with all its might.

All of a sudden, someone was shouting my name and trying to get into the room. 'Who is it?' 'It's Alex!' came the reply and I let him come in. His concern was welcome but it seemed everyone wanted to know what I had done to cause this problem. 'Nothing! I shrieked.

By now the captain had become involved and I was summoned to his cabin to explain what had happened. It was a difficult conversation due to his poor command of English, but I managed to get my story conveyed and it seemed serious enough to make a call to the office in Tel Aviv. The harbour police were contacted and they sent a boat out to the ship where the questioning started again. I was now feeling like a criminal myself, but was pleased to see my attacker taken off the ship by the police and back to land.

What happened to him in the following week, I do not know, but I was amazed when he returned to the m.v. Peace a week later as if nothing had happened. It was decided that he had gone a little mad, having been at sea for over a year without shore leave. My plate banging episode, it would seem, had tipped him over the edge and now apparently fully recovered, he was back on the ship. Needless to say, I mended my ways in the galley and made it a priority to stay well out of his way. I would not temp fate.

CHAPTER 32

Shore leave brought many excursions into unknown territory and a trip to Jerusalem seemed on the cards.

Alex and I had boarded the bus in Tel Aviv at the main terminal along with several armed soldiers on leave, and an assortment of locals. Leave was over for many troops and they were on their way back to barracks, along with tourists and locals visiting family along the route. There was no air-conditioning on many of the buses on this route and as it was so stifling in this middle-eastern heat, I opened as many windows as I could manage from my seat halfway down the bus.

The journey was slow and the stops many as we plied our way through the biblical scenery, sometimes bumping along with such force, I feared for the suspension of the old bus.

There were places where I guessed nothing had changed since the time of Jesus; so many small huts with children playing outside, sometimes running into the fields nearby. I looked out across acres of open land with mules ferrying small payloads along dust-tracks with a weary minder walking alongside, swatting flies on the rump of his animal; this was a scene that hardly changed in many a mile.

At long last we got to the outskirts of Jerusalem and started the long climb into the city. By now I was suffering from the intense heat having finished all my cold drinks, and I longed to get off this contraption.

My disbelief was stretched to breaking point when an old lady leant over me, talking very quickly in Hebrew and starting to close all the windows, the very windows through which I was gasping for air.

Not speaking Hebrew left me at a disadvantage but I made my displeasure more than obvious which brought forth a torrent of what I imagine was sheer indignation on the lady's part. Others joined in and I became more determined to keep my airways free. I opened the window nearest me again and gave her a look of disdain. She reacted immediately with total outrage. I thought she was being awkward for the sake of it, but no; there was an understandable motive for closing the windows.

It was always done along this stretch of the road, as an American tourist explained to me later. Arab boys would quite often sit on roof tops, laughing hysterically, and throw bricks and rocks onto the Israeli buses as they passed slowly below. The toughened glass afforded some obvious protection, but with open windows, we would be inviting injury; the lady had been following protocol. But in my defence, I had been very hot and not aware of the situation. I was foolish and ignorant.

There was so much history to see and understand in Israel. On other shore leaves, I took a boat ride on the Sea of Galilee and visited the River Jordan where Jesus had been baptised by John the Baptist, so many generations before. It left me breathless with wonderment.

The bus ride home was less eventful and the heat not quite so searing. The day ended with a visit to a funfair in Tel Aviv where I proceeded to panic quite seriously on the pirate ship ride when it remained in the vertical position. Alex thought it highly amusing.

The ship swung left to right, increasing the angle each time, but then on an upswing, it appeared to remain in place. Everybody was hanging on for dear life and we stayed there for what felt like an eternity, with children screaming and adults ashen-faced, before we finally swung back to the horizontal, probably within moments. It felt longer, and I wanted to kiss the ground on arrival at terra firma, but thought better of it.

A little later after dinner, it seemed a good idea to saunter along the seafront and nip off to a club run by a very ostentatious creature, named Offer Nissim. He was a star in his little world of club music and played the part with great finesse and flamboyancy. We stood alongside him in his deejay booth as he pandered to the heaving, sweating masses below.

Deejays from the Voice of Peace were always given a special welcome at the club, although it was a two-way street, as we always plugged Offer's club on the air when we got back to the ship.

Several large vodkas later and I was beginning to feel the effects, so it seemed a good idea to struggle the mile or so back to the hotel. This took us through the gay park and the red-light district enabling a choice of entertainment for anyone who may be interested. But not tonight, as I longed for my bed; never was it more welcome.

As my six months in Israel were coming to a close, most of the people I knew on the ship had gone home and more deejays had arrived from England.

So far, the weather had been reasonably okay, but by early winter, things had started to change for the worse and we suffered a particularly severe storm during November, which dragged our ship several miles from her anchorage.

My six month contract was now up and it was time to go home, although I did so with a heavy heart having considered staying another six months. I had fallen in love with Israel and its people; the thought of leaving was a painful wrench, but I would have to go and make a living back in England.

All these months later, back in Europe, the Ross Revenge had remained at sea, off the air with no sign of any comeback on the horizon. I anticipated an uncertain future, but it was one that could not be postponed.

I flew back into Gatwick airport in November, nineteen ninety-one in the middle of a wild storm. The winds were so strong that night that we made two attempts to land, the screaming of the engines powering up again to gain height after the first aborted landing. This caused me to grip the arms of the seat so tightly, my fingers ached for hours afterwards.

The rain lashed the tarmac as I ran from the plane to get inside the terminal, cursing the fact that I had come back to England.

My mind was still in Tel Aviv as I took the Gatwick shuttle into Victoria station. And this is where I stayed for the next seven hours as I waited for the first train to leave for Kent on Sunday morning. No-one is allowed to remain in the station overnight and I was moved out into the street whilst I waited for my train in the howling November storm. I sneaked back into the station several more times before morning, but was moved on each time by ever exasperated policemen. But, unknown to me, there were far worse things happening out in the North Sea.

CHAPTER 33

My return home was met with the same news that I had heard on so many occasions over the years. Radio Caroline's ship had broken her anchor chain in the night and the ship was drifting in wild seas off the Kent coast, with no engines and no spare anchor. It was a very dangerous time for all concerned and could have ended in disaster. The ship was pounded by heavy seas as she lay trapped on the Goodwin Sands. The lifeboat sent to the aid of the crew onboard the Ross Revenge ran aground during the rescue and there was even concern that it had overturned. Thankfully, the crewmen were safe, but the rescue was then carried out from the air.

The crew were airlifted from the ship by the coastguard helicopter and taken ashore, where they awaited the usual questioning by the authorities. As for the ship, she lay grounded on the Goodwin Sands, a notorious graveyard for shipping. The Ross Revenge remained upright and in one piece, an achievement in itself, for no vessel had ever survived such a grounding.

The story played out over several days on the television and radio news as Dover Harbour Board made several attempts to tow the ship to safety. All the efforts paid off in the end and eventually she was towed into Dover where the DTI had a field day searching the ship from stem to stern for all sorts of contraband; none was found, despite their anticipation.

It seemed my return to England had ended my association with offshore radio for ever. I did not go back to the Peaceship to work, although I went back to Israel many times and still have good friends in that country.

Abie Nathan meanwhile, the owner, ran out of money a couple of years later and the station closed down. He decided to sink the ship in the deep Mediterranean waters after many attempts to find a permanent berth.

Abie suffered two strokes in the nineteen-nineties, and sadly died in August, two thousand and eight.

But now I was back in England, and Invicta FM in Kent was my next port of call. There followed work at Essex Radio along with several satellite stations and more local radio work.

But life away from the radio was to take on a different form shortly into the nineties as my mother became increasingly unwell, with Parkinson's Disease taking hold. I became a full-time carer and over the years, looking after her became upsetting and exhausting. Some help was forthcoming from Social Services, but anybody who has dealt with them will know how difficult and trying they can be at times.

After a fall at home, she was taken to the Kent and Canterbury hospital with a broken leg. After many months of pain and several operations, it was announced she could at last return home. But sadly, this was not to be, as she succumbed to the MRSA virus and died in two thousand and one. The inquest recorded a verdict of accidental death.

She had been a great devotee of Radio Caroline and followed the ups and downs of the station with concern and admiration; we had both been passionate about its survival.

Radio Caroline continues to broadcast from land-based studios in Kent, occasionally using the now berthed Ross Revenge. But the magic, the excitement, and sheer unpredictability of the station has gone. It awaits Radio Caroline's return to the high seas to regain that special broadcast sound.

Sadly, this is an unattainable aspiration, and I can only thank God that I had the sheer luck to have been involved in such an important part of broadcasting history.

I met so many notable people over the years, some of them no longer alive, but I remember them with much love and affection.

It was an adventure that will not happen again; real theatre on the radio, real characters living real lives, far out to sea. The highs and lows became intermingled with the lives of listeners, and occasionally routines on land were uniquely fashioned around the broadcasts from the high seas.

The heart and soul of Radio Caroline has been torn out now, and it remains to be seen how radio will develop over the years and whether Caroline will be part of it.

A lot of 'offshore water' has passed under the bridge since the glory days of the radioships and numerous people have forged careers in their chosen profession, thanks to the stations at sea.

I have made many friends over the years thanks to the ships, but I will always remember my days on the Mi Amigo with far more affection than those of the Ross Revenge; my first ship had more character, caused me far less heartache and the people were real friends and remain close. The Ross Revenge produced many memorable broadcasters but I found the camaraderie never quite the same. But maybe it's me!

I do, however, get quiet satisfaction knowing that no government ever forced Radio Caroline from the high seas. Both the Mi Amigo and the

Ross Revenge suffered from an act of God, and as such were victims of bad weather. In the sixties, it was creditors rather than any government that eventually saw off the two Caroline ships.

The Voice of Peace closed down voluntarily and the Cedarlea project in Aberdeen never really got off the ground. Sadly, Radio Paradise was the victim of an illegal Dutch raid.

Fortunately, Radio Caroline survived such an event before the weather closed in on the last beacon of broadcasting freedom from the North Sea.

The End

ADDENDUM

In the 21st century, Radio Caroline continues to broadcast around the world on the internet via the station's website and a variety of mobile apps; all unheard of facilities in the offshore days. Many former Caroline presenters have returned to the current Caroline and with today's technology, programmes can be streamed in from anywhere in the world. The necessities required to operate a radio station have changed beyond recognition since the m.v. Fredericia first dropped anchor off the English coast in 1964.

Today, with a choice of listening once never imagined, some question the point of Radio Caroline. But she has as much right as anyone else to broadcast. We occasionally forget why Ronan O'Rahilly started Caroline in the first place; it was to play music. Music unavailable anywhere else. This is what Radio Caroline strives for today, although no format is exclusive to Caroline anymore. But with so many stations competing for an audience, it is impossible to attain the mass appeal of earlier years and with Radio Caroline broadcasting only on the internet, the task is even more difficult. Talk of an AM licence is often heard but it remains to be seen whether such a thing will become a reality. There are those who, sadly, appear to show antipathy towards such a move and without their approval, nothing will happen.

The Radio Caroline of the 21st century bears little resemblance to the romantic offshore scenarios. This applies to both the broadcasting platform and programming content. But somewhere in the Caroline schedules of today, there are glimpses of former glories; although, sometimes, it does take a while to locate them.

Nonetheless, after all these years, Radio Caroline has managed to survive, and changed broadcasting history in the process. Nobody could have envisaged as those early transmissions got underway in 1964, that so many years later, Caroline would still be broadcasting, only this time, to a worldwide audience.

It's all over now; the Ross Revenge in Dover (1991)

Nigel Harris on land-based radio

Quire; St. Michael's Church, Sittingbourne

The organ console in St. Michael's Church

Ships in Troubled Waters

Printed in Great Britain
by Amazon.co.uk, Ltd.,
Marston Gate.